GUIDE TO MANAGING GROWTH

OTHER ECONOMIST BOOKS

Guide to Analysing Companies
Guide to Business Modelling
Guide to Business Planning
Guide to Economic Indicators
Guide to the European Union
Guide to Financial Management
Guide to Financial Markets
Guide to Hedge Funds
Guide to Investment Strategy
Guide to Management Ideas and Gurus
Guide to Organisation Design
Guide to Project Management
Guide to Supply Chain Management
Numbers Guide
Style Guide

Book of Obituaries
Brands and Branding
Business Consulting
Business Strategy
Buying Professional Services
The City
Coaching and Mentoring
Doing Business in China
Economics
Emerging Markets
Headhunters and How to Use Them
Mapping the Markets
Marketing
Organisation Culture
Successful Strategy Execution
The World of Business

Directors: an A-Z Guide
Economics: an A-Z Guide
Investment: an A-Z Guide
Negotiation: an A-Z Guide

Pocket World in Figures

GUIDE TO MANAGING GROWTH

Turning success into even bigger success

Rupert Merson

THE ECONOMIST IN ASSOCIATION WITH
PROFILE BOOKS LTD

Published by Profile Books Ltd
3a Exmouth House
Pine Street
London EC1R OJH
www.profilebooks.com

Typeset in EcoType by MacGuru Ltd
info@macguru.org.uk

Printed in Great Britain by Clays, Bungay, Suffolk

A CIP catalogue record for this book is available from the British Library

ISBN 978 1 84668 413 5
eISBN 978 1 84765 663 6

Contents

Acknowledgements

AS IS EVIDENT on every page of this book, a huge debt is owed to a wide range of previous thinkers and writers. Where possible acknowledgements have been made directly in the text or in the end-notes. If any have been missed I apologise.

Particular thanks are owed to my fellow faculty members at London Business School from whom I've learned an enormous amount – particularly Keith Willey, with whom I have taught a course called Managing the Growing Business for over ten years, and John Bates, without whom I would not have been at LBS at all.

I would also like to acknowledge the contributions of former colleagues at BDO, particularly Iain Henderson and Don Williams in London, and Maria Karalis in New York.

Lastly, I would like to thank my wife, with whom I have shared this book on too many family holidays.

1 Introduction

MANY NEW OR successful businesses seek to grow, but the achievement of growth can be problematic and requires thoughtful and skilful management, not least because of the many questions it raises. What do we mean by growth? What kind of growth is desirable? How does a business change as it grows? How should owners and managers deal with this change? Is there an optimum rate of growth? Can a business grow too quickly? To what extent can and should managers control the rate of growth in a business? What are the real costs of growth: not just the financial costs, but the personal costs, particularly to those on the inside of the organisation? What are the enablers of growth, and are there levers that managers can pull that will help the business grow further and faster? Is growth itself an inevitable concomitant of success or can you have success without it? Is growth even desirable? What are the barriers to growth? Do the answers to these questions change from industry to industry, from country to country and culture to culture?

Part of the problem when thinking about growth is that those involved have to get used to thinking about organisations as transient things in a permanent state of flux. Many ambitious, younger managers will have experienced walking into a new organisation and quickly forming a view of what is wrong with the place. "When I'm in charge I'll sort out this and correct that and fire him and promote her – and everything will then be fine." But once they are in charge many of these individuals realise that management is not that simple; that problems change even as you attempt to solve them; and that next year's problem is complicated by rather than resolved by last year's solution.

The management of change is never easy, and in a growing business change can be both fast and complex. Even if growth is a consequence of success, it brings organisational challenges that threaten the success that caused it. In order to sustain growth it is important to realise that what worked last year will not necessarily work next year; an organisation that wants to manage growth successfully needs to change things that are not yet broken.

Change inside an organisation is compounded by changes outside it. Indeed, growth in a business itself often triggers change in a market and industry, which in turn demands further change in the business. Growth may attract competitors, competing technologies and regulators, as well as customers from different markets with different expectations.

Growth gives rise to problems for businesses of all sizes. Different divisions in a big business evolve at different speeds and may be at different stages of their evolution, each with its own problems – with the additional problem for the organisation as a whole that the plans of the divisions be satisfactorily reconciled with each other. Mergers, joint ventures and acquisitions – different routes for getting big – bring other challenges, not least with integration. Small businesses have different sorts of growth challenges as they seek to establish credibility as well as culture, brand and identity, develop secure lines of supply and sustainable relationships with customers and financiers, and manage the changing relationship between owners and managers. An established business in one country investing in a small venture in another needs to acknowledge not just the legal and cultural differences between the two countries, but also the differences between managing a large, corporate business and a small entrepreneurial firm.

Businesses that fail to manage growth become its victims. Some businesses go bust, not for lack of potential, but because they fail to manage the consequences of the growth they have achieved. Growth has many implications for a business, not least the financial pressures it can bring.

Summarised like this it is amazing that any business bothers growing at all. Indeed, most do not. Figure 1.1 shows that, of just over 5m businesses registered in the United States as having any employees

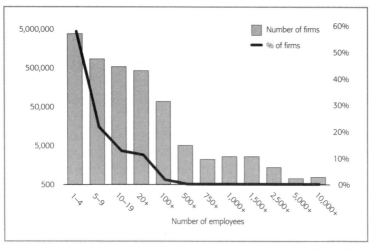

Source: US Census Bureau

FIG 1.1 Number of firms categorised by number of employees, United States, 2002

throughout 2002, almost 2,800,000 (almost 56%) had fewer than five. As a percentage of all businesses, those with more than 500 employees scarcely register on the graph. Of course, there are thousands of small businesses around the world, many of which no doubt provide satisfactory returns to those who run them, who have no wish for the business to grow.

However, for every business that is content with its current size, there are many with ambitions to grow. This book is for them. It argues that businesses that anticipate and manage the challenges of growth give themselves the best chance of ensuring growth is secure and sustainable. It draws on the thinking of academics and business people as well as the experience of those working in business in its aim to help managers in their pursuit of growth. It covers all the aspects involved – strategy, performance measurement and management, people management, sales and marketing, finance – and it takes into account differences in business size, sector and location.

2 Stages of growth

WHEN BUSINESSES GROW they do not just get bigger. They also change to become qualitatively and quantitatively different. The change involves many dimensions and many stages in what is a never-ending journey.

Leadership versus management

As a first step towards conceptualising the stages businesses pass through as they grow it is useful to consider the difference between those who start new businesses and those who run big ones. Abraham Zaleznik, emeritus professor of leadership at Harvard Business School, in 1977 was one of the earliest management writers to have drawn a distinction between creative, inspirational and enthusiastic types, and organised, disciplined, sensible managerial types, using the labels "leader" for the former and "manager" for the latter (see Figure 2.1). It is a distinction that has also been usefully applied to entrepreneurs and other members of the management team of new businesses.

Most businesses start high on leadership and low on management. (John Kotter uses the matrix shown in Figure 2.1 to contrast leadership and management in his 1996 book *Leading Change*.) If they are to stand a chance of developing into something that is remotely sustainable, they will need more of the qualities of energy, inspiration and creativity. A business in its early stages will thus move from 1 to 2 if it is to evolve, dominated by individuals with qualities of leadership. Organisation, management and governance in these early stages are as much to do with force of personality as anything else. The

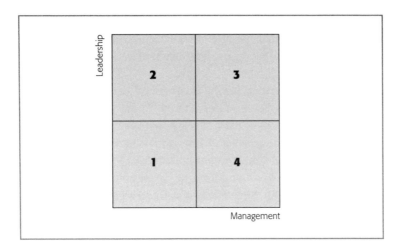

FIG 2.1 The leadership/management matrix

organisation hardly exists at all, and the business is wholly identified with its founders and owners.

But things change. As Jeremy Newman, former CEO of BDO International, wrote in "Leadership and Management", in the *Journal of Business Growth and Profitability*, in 1997:

> New businesses are started by entrepreneurs who, through some combination of wisdom and luck, create and implement a successful business strategy. The business expands and profits grow and with this comes the need to hire professional managers. So people are recruited and promoted to manage, to cope with the growing bureaucracy and to prevent things getting out of control. And so the organisation grows and management grows to cope with it.

The introduction of "management" heralds reporting timetables, appraisal schemes, formal agendas and other manifestations of the way to run a proper business. From an organisation that thrives on the high octane of entrepreneurship and rushing around after the next sale, the new business inevitably evolves into one in which disciplined forces of management have far more influence. The business moves from 2 to 3, where leadership and management styles are in balance, which is the ideal position for the senior team. There is enough business discipline and governance to sustain the business, but not too much so that the qualities of entrepreneurship and leadership are damaged.

For many businesses, staying in 3 sounds good in theory but is difficult to achieve. Some entrepreneurs ("leaders") feel obliged to turn into managers, or at least develop management capability. But although people can change and develop, it is rare to find an individual who can operate comfortably at both ends of the leadership/management spectrum. Changing from being an entrepreneur to being CEO or chairman of a big business is difficult, as Stelios Haji-Iannou indicated when resigning as chairman of easyJet in April 2002:[1]

> *Starting a company requires a very different skill-set from those needed to chair a major plc, and I consider my strengths are in the former. The history of the City is littered with entrepreneurs who held on to their creations for too long, failing to recognise the changing needs of the company.*

Rather than take on the managerial role themselves, entrepreneurs may best serve their own and their business's interests by seeking to recruit the necessary management expertise. But in doing this, entrepreneurs should realise that their role is still likely to need to change. Entrepreneurs and their new managers may not to see to eye-to-eye, and an entrepreneur who does not adapt to the new organisational circumstances is heading for conflict with the new management team. This often results in damage to the business and the departure of one or the other. Indeed, a reluctance to face up to the consequences of the tension leads some businesses to duck the problem in the first place. But businesses must introduce a management infrastructure if they are serious about sustainable growth. Family businesses are particularly prone to deferring the necessary professionalisation of management.

Many people with a managerial bent assume that the management force is more important than the entrepreneurial one. Indeed, this is a tendency in much business thinking. As Newman says:

This in turn stifles leadership and encourages management and because the business is successful, managers begin to believe that they are the best and their idiosyncrasies become part of the culture of the organisation.

Although it is true that a business without decent management will not survive for long, a business in which the management impulse takes over and the entrepreneurial spirit is squeezed out will become yet another overmanaged, underinspired, middle-aged business on a glide-path to history. Premature ageing in an organisation is almost as worrying as a refusal to let it grow up. This is a feature of start-ups established by large companies, as a result of the mistaken assumption that a small business is just a small version of a big one. In the case of a stand-alone joint venture established by two UK listed companies (one a retailer, the other a broadcaster), the new chief executive was keen to "establish an entrepreneurial culture" but said that his first priority was to discuss implementing a defined-benefit pension scheme. This is a sure sign of a business on its way to being old before its time. That it is common for the finance director to succeed the entrepreneur as chief executive in a growing business would seem to illustrate how the discipline of accountancy can supersede the energy and creativity and propensity to take risk. A survey of FTSE 100 CEOs in 2010 found that over half of them had strong financial backgrounds.

As well as highlighting a contrast between the entrepreneur and the more managerially and governance-minded members of a team, the leadership/management model outlines what is for many businesses a feature of the history of their growth and development. The model is primarily about different types of people, but indirectly it describes the stages that all businesses have to pass through as they evolve, and how the managerial, organisational, strategic and operational imperatives differ significantly from one stage to the next. In short, as well as growing, businesses have to grow up. The leadership/management model just hints at stages of evolution companies have to pass through. But there are plenty of thinkers who have taken their analysis much further.

Modelling growth

When those who study growth attempt to structure their thinking the result is often a "growth model", an analytic framework that describes the stages that businesses pass through as they evolve, the characteristics of each stage, and the changes necessary to facilitate the move of the company from one stage to the next. The remainder of this chapter outlines the best-known growth models and explores how useful they are to those trying to grow their businesses or deal with the consequences of growth.

Evolution and revolution: the Greiner model

Larry E. Greiner, Professor of Management and Organisation at the Marshall School of Business at the University of Southern California, published his article "Evolution and Revolution as Organisations Grow" in *Harvard Business Review* in 1972. It is not the first model, but it is the oldest one still in common use. It describes five phases of growth through which businesses pass. In 1998 Greiner revised his model, adding a sixth stage.

Greiner outlines five developmental phases of company growth. Although each phase starts with a period of evolution, it ends in revolution, a period of "substantial organisational turmoil and change". How the revolutionary period is resolved determines whether or not the organisation will develop further.

The periods of revolution are at the heart of the model. Greiner's notion of revolution draws attention to the inevitability of change in the development of an organisation. The "critical task" for management in each revolutionary period is to find the new set of practices that will become the basis of managing the next period of evolutionary growth. But in so doing managers "experience the irony of seeing a major solution in one period become a major problem in a later period".

The five phases are as follows:

■ **Creativity.** In the phase of creativity, the founder's energies are consumed by doing rather than managing and decisions are taken quickly and reactively. It ends in a crisis of leadership, in which the business addresses the question of who will establish

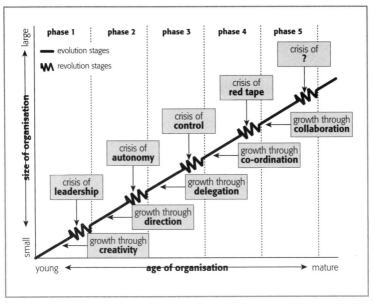

Source: Larry Greiner, "Evolution and Revolution as Organisations Grow", *Harvard Business Review*, 1972

FIG 2.2 Greiner's five-phase model

some necessary order in the chaos. Resolution of the crisis might well involve the recruitment of a "capable business manager".

■ **Direction.** The first revolution will be followed by a phase of direction, in which management systems and processes are introduced and developed and communication and management become more formal. As the organisation grows, however, such systems, designed initially to support growth, end up constricting it. There is a crisis of autonomy, in which middle managers are "torn between following procedures and taking initiative on their own".

■ **Delegation.** The second revolution is resolved by the establishment and development of a more decentralised structure in a phase of delegation, during which senior executives manage by exception and junior managers have budget and profit responsibility for divisions and departments.

But the revolution, a "crisis of control", occurs when senior executives sense that they are losing control of a business with more and more offshoots. For some a re-imposition of central control is the obvious way forward.

- **Co-ordination.** However, going backwards is never an option for a business with ambition. The third revolution results in a phase of co-ordination, in which senior managers use formal systems for achieving co-ordination. Some functions are centralised, capital expenditure is carefully controlled, formal planning processes are established, and share options and company-wide bonus schemes may be used to "encourage employees to identify with the organisation as a whole". This focus on systems and co-ordination ends in a crisis of red tape, in which "procedures take precedence over problem solving".

- **Collaboration.** The fourth revolution results in a phase of collaboration in which teamwork, social control and self-discipline replace "formal control". The focus shifts from process to problem solving, and from headquarters to interdisciplinary teams. Matrix structures (see page 78) are established to balance and resolve the competing thinking of different interest groups. Above all, there is a shift from individuals and systems to the collective.

Greiner, in his first article on the subject, said that he did not know how phase five would end (although he later suggested a sixth phase – see below). He imagines that the revolution "will centre around the psychological saturation of employees who grow emotionally and physically exhausted from the intensity of teamwork and the heavy pressure for innovative solutions". He imagines organisations with structures that allow employees to "rest, reflect and revitalise them-selves". He imagines organisations making more use of sabbaticals, and balancing structured work and reflection. In so doing, Greiner is attempting to describe not so much the next phase of growth of businesses in general but the organisation of the future. Thus Greiner is one of the first to discover what many writers about growth have subsequently discovered, though few have been as honest as him in acknowledging, that the early phases of growth are a lot easier to describe and analyse than the later phases.

Greiner is also unusual in being allowed to be his own best critic. His 1972 piece was reprinted as a *Harvard Business Review* classic in 1998. In his comments on his own work after an interval of 26 years it is phase five that comes in for the most robust criticism. He suggests that his "speculation that 'psychological saturation' is the crisis ending phase five now seems wrong", and that the crisis is likely to be the realisation that there is no longer an internal solution. To keep growing the organisation needs to look outside itself – for partners, or maybe for "opportunities to sell itself to a bigger company". Indeed, Greiner suggests that maybe there is a sixth phase of growth dependent on such "extra-organisational solutions", and gives GE as an example of an organisation in which a group of companies have been built up around a core.

His model is presented as a series of hypotheses. Greiner reminds us that in the original article "the phases outlined ... are merely five in number and are still only approximations". The article always was an invitation to others to test, refine and, in all likelihood, correct if not contradict his work. Though many have worked on growth, Greiner's model still serves as the standard against which all others are judged.

Does Greiner's version of growth have any practical utility for managers? Greiner thinks so, though his "explicit guidelines for managers in growing organisations to keep in mind" are modest. Managers, he argues, benefit from knowing where they are in the development sequence and therefore understand when the time to act has come. His model implies that managers should recognise the limited range of their own solutions. Managers' interventions are time and context specific. No matter how good they were last year, next year a different phase might start, with a different set of problems. Greiner argues, after all, that the problems of one revolution are sown like seeds in the solutions to a previous revolution.

Greiner's analysis has a lot to commend it. Business leaders do indeed find it useful to plot their business against Greiner's model, using it to help understand the problems it survived last year and anticipate what might be around the corner. The focus on revolution and crisis is also useful. Too many managers assume that business problems need solving only once. Greiner reminds us that in a growing business in particular yesterday's solutions become tomorrow's problems; in an ambitious, successful business, continuous change is necessary. If nothing appears to be wrong, ask yourself whether you are looking in the right place. The model also draws attention to the pain that growth brings. If you are ambitious and choose to grow your business, you need to acknowledge the problems you will encounter.

The model's simplicity is beguiling to many of those attempting to anticipate and prepare for the changes that growth will bring, but some find it frustrating and unnaturally deterministic. Cynics might see the oscillation between revolution and evolution as a reflection of the times in which the model was created (the early 1970s), with the barriers not long down outside the Sorbonne and Marxism taken much more seriously in academic and political circles than at any time since. Greiner writes about the importance of "the forces of history" and notes that he has "drawn from the legacies of European psychologists who argue that the behaviour of individuals is determined primarily by past events and experiences rather than by what lies ahead". Indeed, he is dismissive of managers who "fix their gaze outward on the environment and toward the future, as if more precise market projections will provide the organisation with a new identity". But context is crucial, and a manager who attempts to manage without paying attention to it is risking much. Besides, Greiner himself took to speculating about the future even while trying to outline the characteristics of the later phases of the model. He is right when he suggests that managers should pay attention to the influence of "past decisions", although he is perhaps unfair in suggesting that these matter more than "present events or market dynamics". In the real world business leaders need to plan, and planning involves an understanding of the present as well as some anticipation of what the future holds, both in the market place and in the company. Business plans are discussed in Chapter 4.

Small business growth: the Churchill model

Neil Churchill is Emeritus Professor of Entrepreneurship at INSEAD in France and has been a distinguished member of the faculty of other institutions. His *Five Stages of Small Business Growth* was first published by Harvard Business School in 1983, and has been much revised since. Churchill, together with his co-author Virginia Lewis, was conscious of being just one in a line of theorists; he explicitly mentions the work of five previous thinkers, including Greiner. Churchill takes the thinking further, testing his original hypotheses against 83 responses to a questionnaire distributed to 110 owners and managers of successful small companies who had participated in a small-company management programme. They had also read Greiner's article and had identified "as best they could" the stages in Greiner's model that they had passed through.

Churchill is a believer in growth models. When looking at the growth of small businesses, "points of similarity can be organised into a framework that increases our understanding of the nature, characteristics and problems of businesses". Such frameworks can help "in anticipating the key requirements at various points", and can provide bases "for evaluating the impact of present and proposed governmental regulations and policies on one's business". Frameworks can also "aid accountants and consultants in diagnosing problems and matching solutions to smaller enterprises".

Churchill has the experience of testing his hypotheses empirically. He points out that growth can be difficult to pin down – growth of what? Too many business leaders think only in terms of turnover and headcount, but complexity of product line, rate of change in products or production technology, number of locations and so on are also important. Churchill is right, though the challenge of framework and model making is always to strike the right balance between simplification and complexity. Too close to the former will result in the model failing to reflect the messy business that is reality; too close to the latter will render the framework unusable. Churchill also challenged the "grow-or-fail hypothesis implicit in the [Greiner] model". Businesses "plateaued ... with some marginally profitable and others very profitable over a period of between 5 and 80 years". He noted that several of his research subjects were not start-ups but were companies purchased while in a "steady-state survival or success stage" which were then moved further along the growth model thanks to a new attitude (and capability) on the part of new owners and managers.

Like Greiner, on whose work his is based, Churchill describes five phases. He has little truck with Greiner's crises, however, and his phases are presented as discrete stages of evolution:

- **Existence.** In the first stage the organisation is fighting for customers and meeting customer needs. Businesses cannot stay at this stage; they get to stage two or they fail.

- **Survival.** The business has shown that it works, but its main concern is still to cover its costs. In corporate terms it is eking out a subsistence living. Many businesses stay at this stage, including, Churchill argues, "Mom and Pop stores ... [and] manufacturing businesses that cannot get their product or process sold as planned".

- **Success.** In the first version of his model Churchill calls the third stage the success stage. The business is established and sustainable, and this success offers the owner alternatives. The success stage comes in two forms. III-G is the "success-growth substage", during which the owner throws the dice again in pursuit of further growth. Such a path is inherently risky; the owner might lose. III-D is the "success-disengagement substage". Rather than throw the dice again, the owner chooses to take a step back and live off the cash generated by the business, trusting management to run the business conservatively. On the assumption that the economic environment is stable, Churchill sees no reason why a business might not stay in the III-D phase for a long time.

- **Take-off.** A business owner who chooses to throw the dice again in stage III-G and succeeds will reach stage four, which Churchill calls take-off. He talks about the owner's ability to delegate; the ability of the business to generate sufficient cash to satisfy growth; and operational and strategic planning. At this stage the founder might have left the business.

- **Resource-maturity.** The prize for the successful negotiation of stage four is stage five, called resource-maturity. This is the phase inhabited by bigger, stable businesses. Businesses in stage five need to "consolidate and control the financial gains brought on by rapid growth" while retaining "the advantages of small size, including flexibility of response and the entrepreneurial spirit". The biggest danger is that the entrepreneurial spirit will be crushed as management expands. Churchill suggests that there might be a sixth phase called ossification but does not develop his thinking.

Although Churchill was hugely influenced by Greiner, his thinking differs significantly. Churchill recognises that businesses have options. For Greiner, businesses are set on a historically predetermined path. The pace of change might vary, but the sequence of stages is almost pre-destined. Churchill allows more room for choice. Indeed, stage three of his original model presents the alternatives III-G and III-D – growth or disengagement. This might not be considered a choice at all, rather a sensible recognition that many business leaders, like most players of Monopoly, will choose to give up playing the game rather than see it through to its later stages. That many business leaders choose not to throw the dice again does not introduce flexibility into the model. Indeed, in later versions, Churchill replaces the alternatives III-G and III-D with a more conventional stage three leading to stage four.

Although at first glance it may not seem so, Churchill's model is much more complicated than Greiner's. Introducing alternatives and choices will complicate any model. Churchill also discusses management factors identified in his research that change in importance as a business passes from one stage to the next. Four of these are related to the company itself: financial, personnel, systems and business resources. Four others are associated with the owner: personal goals, operational abilities, management abilities and strategic abilities. Churchill attempts to wrestle with many more variables than Greiner does. On the one hand this reflects the diversity of the real businesses that lie behind his thinking; on the other hand it makes the model less easy to apply by managers interested in the fates of their own businesses.

As already indicated, Churchill has over the years made revisions to his model, including the radical replacement of the choice between III-G and III-D. That his thinking has evolved shows how difficult it can be to generalise about how businesses change as they grow.

An anthropomorphic approach: the Adizes model

Ichak Adizes takes a very different approach to growth from both Greiner and Churchill. Adizes was a member of the faculty of UCLA until 1982, when he founded the Adizes Institute.

Adizes, who outlines his approach in his 1999 book *Managing Corporate Lifecycles*, is unusual in that he envisages a ten-stage corporate life cycle charting the life of a business not just from birth to success, but also from success to death. His stages are as follows (the labels are his but the descriptions in brackets are the author's):

1. Courtship (the creation of the organisation)

2. Infancy (the commencement of trading)

3. Go-go (energetic early growth with the chaos that can result)

4. Adolescence (the organisation is established but still evolving fast and has recently established an identity independent of its founders)

5. Prime (the organisation has reached its "prime of life" and is therefore at its fittest, most competitive, and profitable)

6. Stability (though still effective, and often still profitable, the signs of decline are beginning to appear even if they are not properly acknowledged)

7. Aristocracy (few doubt that the organisation has a powerful place in the market, but it is viewed as inflexible and conservative; nimble new market entrants are beginning to take market share, and maybe market trends are changing, leaving the organisation behind)

8. Early bureaucracy (called "recrimination" in some versions of the model – even the organisation itself acknowledges that something is wrong; doubts and internal squabbles distract attention from customer service and the objectives of the organisation)

9. Bureaucracy (attention is focused inwards as the organisation struggles to stay alive; any outward attention is directed at possible exits or the sale of the organisation)

10. Death (or rather the commercial equivalent – one of the various forms of bankruptcy, or protection from bankruptcy – receivership, administration, liquidation – or perhaps sale for break-up.)

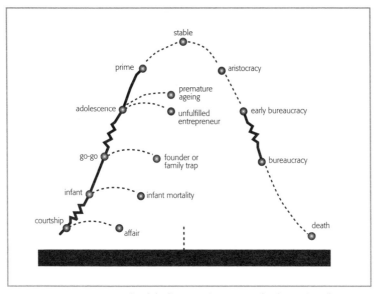

Source: After Ichak Adizes, *Managing Corporate Lifecycles*, Prentice Hall Press, 1999

FIG 2.3 The Adizes model

It is the road to "prime" that matters most to Adizes, and making the changes necessary to keeping your organisation there once you have achieved it.

As Figure 2.3 illustrates, there are several places where Adizes suggests the business can fail. He also uses distinctive language – the language of human development. Adizes is not the only thinker to liken the growth of an organisation to the growth of a human being. Indeed, it can be difficult not to slip into anthropomorphic metaphors when discussing the evolution of the business. Some writers go further – Greiner noted the influence on his thinking of the "legacies of European psychologists". But Adizes is distinctive in the extent to which he pushes the analogy.

Undoubtedly, many business founders are comfortable with this sort of thinking, often adopting parent/child-style relationships with the businesses they have created. Their attachment can often seem irrational – for example, when it comes to selling equity in the business, more than one business founder has likened it to selling your children. The risk, of course, when applying the analogy to a growth framework, is one of oversimplification.

The DIAMOND model

The DIAMOND model was created by partners and staff at the London office of BDO Stoy Hayward, now BDO LLP, a global accountancy network. The creators of the model reviewed and critically evaluated the published literature and then tested the resulting hypothetical framework against the experience of the firm's clients. The aim was to synthesise the best of the rest, and produce something business leaders and their advisers could use (see Figure 2.4).

The model envisages seven stages in the growth of a business:

D **Dreaming** up the idea of a new business, developing plans and defining start-up requirements.

I **Initiating** the business plan and inspiring others in order to establish a presence in the market. This is the implementation of the dream.

A **Attacking** the first problems of growth and coping with adolescence. During this stage the business has the ability to survive and it can provide a good living for its owners. However, it is not robust enough to sustain a major change in its market or operating environment, and its cash flow and customer base limit its long-term prospects. As a business passes through this stage, the pressures of growth accelerate. Wise and well-advised owners recognise that although the business has succeeded so far, it will not be sustainable for long if it does not anticipate the next stage. For others, failing to recognise and react to the pressure to grow up organisationally can lead to a gradual loss of control, and to accumulating pressures that lead to anxiety rather than action and result in stagnation and even failure.

M **Maturing** the business with an emphasis on establishing controls, systems and methodologies. Management is professionalised to deal with the size and complexity of the customer base or the organisational structure of the business.

O **Overhauling** the organisation with a clear focus on objectives. The business is more competitive and has a strong customer and

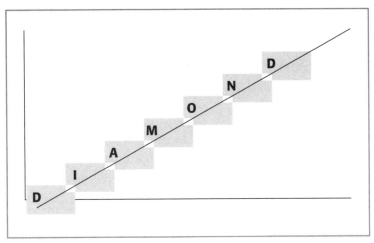

Source: BDO LLP

FIG 2.4 The DIAMOND model

marketing orientation, but there is a sense that something has been lost after years of going for growth and a consequent yearning to recapture the spirit of the business at start-up – or at least to recapture the essence of entrepreneurship that at times seems threatened by necessary disciplines of control. There has to be, in short, a reaction against the tendency to overmanage and stifle creativity and enterprise if the business is to make it big time.

N Networking the units of the business. Strategic processes have become as important as tactical ones. Maintaining and developing a corporate image are important and, by now, earnings are often being managed for a diverse stakeholder group. The personality of the business – its "culture" – is now more influential than the personality of the entrepreneur who founded it.

D Diversifying into new products and markets. Driving growth through strategic alliances and commercial interdependencies that enable rapid responses to market opportunities in a fast-changing world. The culture of organisations in this stage is highly focused. The means by which they operate – and the markets in which they choose to do so – are highly flexible. The rate of growth, year on year, often decelerates as a function of the size of the business. This stage also implies a return to the start, the establishment of new businesses within the business in the search for renewal and product development – entrepreneurship reborn as intrapreneurship.

The use of the DIAMOND mnemonic indicates how far the model has moved from the world of academia and towards that of practical applicability. If it wants to be used, it needs to be remembered.

Other features of the model come from practical experience. Unlike the models discussed so far, the stages, though discrete, overlap. There are echoes of Greiner's crises here, but DIAMOND takes them further, turning crises into "transitional issues", and envisaging that businesses can be in more than one stage of evolution at the same time, and that to presume otherwise is simplistic. Figure 2.5 shows that growth is not linear. It is possible for a business to exhibit the characteristics of more than one stage of growth at a time.

Greiner's crises in part are a product of the tension between two adjacent stages of evolution, with the problems of the later stage sown in the solutions to the earlier stage. Churchill, when discussing management factors, notes that the skills and qualities required for addressing the problems in one stage of evolution are less relevant to another stage, implying that it is potentially a problem if a business cannot be tidily allocated to one stage of evolution or another.

Some advisers working with real businesses have taken these worries further. A UK clearing bank put together a training programme for managers servicing small and medium-sized businesses to impart knowledge of the problems those customers faced. It also prepared a set of diagnostic tools, including an exercise based on Churchill's model, requiring managers to assess which stage of growth a customer might be in. If a business exhibited characteristics typical of more than one stage, the diagnostic tool invited managers to consider whether that customer might be a credit risk to the bank.

Although the bank was instilling knowledge in its staff about the distinctive issues that might affect smaller businesses, its interpretation of the implications of a business exhibiting different stages of growth at the same time is questionable. Real businesses use growth models to help them understand challenges and to address them, but

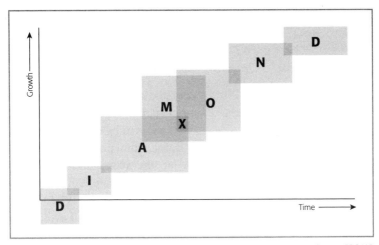

Source: BDO LLP

FIG 2.5 Overlapping stages on the DIAMOND model

invariably real businesses are too complicated to be tidied into one box or another on a model. There are real estate agents with an "eat what you kill" culture that have sophisticated selling and marketing systems but rudimentary HR processes. The imbalance here is recognised and indeed fostered by the senior managers. This is the sort of business they want to run. Then there is the company seeking to innovate. A separate subsidiary has been established for the purpose of taking the new service to market. The subsidiary and its parent are at different stages of evolution; at the same time, both parts of the company need to take advantage of the ties that bind them. Some might argue that each part of the business needs its own model. But this fails to acknowledge the entity in aggregate.

The DIAMOND framework has another characteristic that betrays its supposed genesis in the real world. In reality, business leaders are rarely interested in plotting the history of their businesses, and the implication of some of the models covered in this chapter is that this is where a business manager should start. Whether their business was in stage three or phase A between 2009 and 2011, or whether the crisis of autonomy took place in 2007 or 2008, are questions of historical interest. Only if they can shed light on the problems that need

Table 2.1 The DIAMOND framework

Dominant business perspectives	Dreaming	Initiating	Attacking
Owner focus	Do I have what it takes?	Robust corporate structure Shareholder agreements, etc	Giving up some equity
Management focus	Business plan Market research Seed funding	Cash flow Winning new business Establishing a presence	Cash flow Establishing stability
Finance source	Finding an angel Friends and family	Own equity Angel Clearing bank Cash management	Short-term debt New equity participants Factoring
Investor focus	What else will they bring other than money?	Meeting their targets Taking advantage of their experience	Sufficient returns
Employee focus	–	Excitement versus security	Overworked Growing with job
Marketing and sales focus	Developing contacts Piloting concept	Generating demand Developing distribution channels	Improving customer quality Broadening customer base
IT focus	Planning basic requirements	Off-the-shelf, simple solutions	Reliable systems
Supply-side focus	Establishing contacts Setting quality/cost standards	Ad hoc, experimental	Negotiating long-term relationships
Community focus	Personal	Local employment	Random charitable, local business associations

Maturing	Overhauling	Networking	Diversifying
Establishing formal corporate governance	Possible exit MBO/MBI	Diverse stakeholder group	Diverse stakeholder group
Professional, disciplined management control	Addressing balance between leadership and management Refocusing on objectives	Managing corporate image Managing strategy Joint ventures and alliances	Improving brand value Alliances International expansion New products
Structured finance Long-term debt	Structured finance Venture capital	Venture capital Finance markets	Finance markets
Developing finance strategy	Restricted return for future growth	Retaining stability Maximising returns	Brand equity Shareholder value
Professional management	Incentive based Emphasis on empowerment Options/equity reward	Career development	Moving around the business for new experience
Well-established relationships with range of clients Focusing on repeat business	Focus Brand development	Corporate positioning Brand management	Customer relationship management Brand extension
Bespoke systems for competitive advantage	Re-engineering systems to meet business need	E-commerce Intranet	Knowledge management CRM systems
Multiple supplier management	Rationalising supply Power bargaining	Suppliers as partners	Vertical chain strategies Suppliers in strategic alliances
Focused charitable and community spending	Focused Reinforcing brand	Focused Reinforcing brand	Political influence

Dominant business perspectives	Dreaming	Initiating	Attacking
Transitional issues	Overcoming gaps in knowledge Establishing business focus Company formation Securing finance Obtaining premises Sourcing stock/ suppliers Improving quality of business plan Developing knowledge of market Are founders inventors or entrepreneurs? Can they do it on their own?	Basic systems for income and expenditure Basic systems for meeting customer/ client promises Lack of focus Understanding the extent to which growth consumes cash Identifying need for and recruiting new members of senior team Dealing with the unforeseen – with little experience or skill Not really understanding the customer Dealing with first reactions from the competition Ignoring IT	Not robust enough to survive major change Identifying skill deficiencies Need to introduce professional management apparent No contingency planning Communication lines stretched or inadequate Constrained by initial systems selection Overdependence on founding team Failure to analyse and plan scientifically

to be addressed imminently are they of interest now. Greiner, as has been seen, tries to change this mindset, encouraging managers to look back into history for insight into today's problems. Even if he is right, managers are rarely persuaded. The DIAMOND framework addresses this by attempting to put more flesh on each of the stages, breaking them down into different dimensions, and inviting managers to consider in more detail the implications of the stage of growth their business happens to be in at present.

Once the present condition of the business is understood, attention can be given to changes necessary to prepare the business for the future. The DIAMOND framework attempts to address this by presenting "transitional issues".

The final stage of the model: re-creation

All models are weakest in their final stage. DIAMOND's networking and diversifying stages echo Greiner's new stage 6, which he speculated about some 16 years after the publication of his first model,

Maturing	Overhauling	Networking	Diversifying
Management surpassing leadership Can founders evolve with their business? Losing entrepreneurial spirit Losing touch with the market Increasing lack of organisational flexibility Inappropriate performance indicators Executives not incentivised or motivated correctly Innovation dampened	Business could run away with its own success Overemphasis on management threatens to destroy leadership spirit Overpromise/under-deliver Burn out (people and concept) Lack of corporate governance Culture still immature – in need of further attention Brand management	Business too large to be responsive to change European/economic/export issues Management of overseas subsidiaries High turnover of good staff Sophisticated management hierarchy Pressure from within to start new businesses Development and extension of the brand	–

but they both seem weak and undefined. Churchill leaves us with a mature business with the threat of ossification on the horizon. Greiner's last stage is still, despite his rethinking, left as a big question mark.

It is as if thinkers believe that although it is possible to determine the early phases businesses go through as they grow (not that they can agree what these early phases look like), thereafter businesses have to find their own and different ways.

Some have attempted to wrestle with the final stage more seriously. Adizes suggests that "prime" is a state to be achieved by big businesses and then sustained through a process of perpetual transformation – from which the only other way is down. Another model encourages managers to invest time in developing business systems and, particularly, brand and organisational culture in these later stages.[2] And at least one other model, from Denmark, suggests that it is more helpful to think of growth as a wheel and to consider the end of business evolution to be a process of re-creation, with the last stage in a successful business containing the seeds of new businesses which end up demanding their own growth models. In part, re-creation is implied in DIAMOND's overhauling stage, in Churchill's III-G stage and in all Greiner's revolutions. All these models imply a concern about losing sight of the beginnings of the business and the importance of attempting to reconnect with these.

Horizons of growth

One book that considers re-creation in the context of growth more seriously than most is *The Alchemy of Growth* by Merhdad Baghai, Steve Coley and David White, three McKinsey consultants.[3] Rather than model growth as a series of stages of evolution, they talk about three horizons of growth and consider the growth challenges of an established business.

Horizon one is the core of the business. It might not be growing particularly fast, but without it the business would not exist. It is where the business started and continues to define its identity. Instead of being run with an eye on aggressive expansion, the business is run for profit. Efficiency and quality are crucial. In a large accounting firm, horizon one activity might include auditing and tax compliance advice.

Horizon two is less predictable, not least because it is a newer line of business activity. Sometimes the business makes excellent profits out of horizon two activity, but sometimes it makes significant losses. New business is less certain. In horizon one, new business is attracted because of the long-standing reputation of the organisation, but it cannot rely on this for horizon two. In a large accounting firm, horizon two activity might include corporate finance advice.

Horizon three includes experimentation in new lines of business, few if any of which make money immediately. But this does not mean that horizon three should not be taken seriously. Indeed, Baghai, Coley and White argue that a mature business if it is to grow and thrive rather than shrink needs to be active in all three horizons, which have a symbiotic relationship with each other. Horizons two and three will help keep horizon one fresh; horizons two and three might turn into new horizon ones in the future. In a large accounting firm, there is always investment in new lines of advice and service, for example in management consultancy and tax planning, of which some will turn into profitable businesses while others wither on the vine.

In a successful business, therefore, the three horizons are not static. Baghai, Coley and White cite, for example, Village Roadshow, an Australian company. Until the 1980s its core horizon one activity was operating local cinemas; the development of a national cinema chain was a horizon two investment along with movie distribution, but the business was already investing in horizon three ideas such as multiplex cinemas and theme parks. By the late 1980s, however, movie distribution had moved into horizon one, theme parks and multiplexes had moved into horizon two, while in horizon three the company was exploring cinemas in Asia as well as TV and film production. By the 1990s, theme parks had moved into horizon one, multiplex cinemas remained in horizon two, and new businesses including entertainment centres and retail stores were being explored in horizon three.

To succeed in all the horizons it is important to recognise that each needs managing in its own way, with different performance measures and different incentives (see Chapter 7). It is unlikely that horizon one people will naturally turn successfully to horizon three activity, or vice versa. Indeed, in a large accounting firm someone who is good at new product development, thinking up new solutions for clients, and excited at winning new business is unlikely to be the best person to lead audit assignments, or would be wasted if given that role. Some of these skills might well be useful in horizon one – hence the importance of the symbiotic relationship of the horizons – but in a post-Enron world, accountancy firms have needed to think carefully about these links; and where they have not thought, the regulators have thought for them.

Rethinking the dimensions of growth

When defining the stages of growth, the devisers of models tend to assume that the axes against which growth is plotted are time and size. Even this assumption can be challenged:

- **Time.** Businesses evolve at different speeds. If they pass through the different stages of evolution, they will not do so at the same speed. The time spent in different stages depends on external factors as well as the ambitions and skills of the management team. In businesses that are growing particularly fast, it may be possible to pass through some of the early stages simultaneously, or perhaps miss some of them out altogether.

- **Size.** The obvious question is size of what? Businesses grow in many dimensions. Many managers, particularly those who have grown their businesses from nothing and have successfully attracted new customers and clients, can be seduced into thinking that sales revenue is the obvious measure of size. External shareholders, however, might prefer to measure profit, or returns to investors. Without profit the business will ultimately run out of the capacity to invest; without returns to investors it will run out of capital. There are many examples of businesses that have increased their profits by reducing their turnover. (These financial measures are discussed in Chapter 5.) What about employee headcount as a measure of size? Certainly there is a connection between the size of the workforce and the extent of the management challenge. But the same is true of the extent of any critical resource.

When considering the evolution of new businesses, Amar Bhidé, a professor at the Fletcher School of Law and Diplomacy at Tufts University, focuses less on time and size and pays more attention to risk and irreducible uncertainty, and the relationship of these with profit. In so doing he creates a three-dimensional model of growth (see Figure 2.6).

Bhidé, however, is really drawing attention to a separate factor that changes as organisations evolve from start-up to sustainable business: their appetite for and attitude to risk and the relationship between this and the resources at the disposal of the organisation and planning processes (see Chapters 3 and 4).

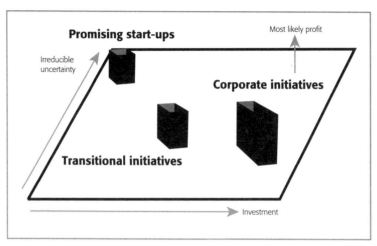

Source: Amar Bhidé, *The Origin and Evolution of New Businesses*, New Oxford University Press, 2000

FIG 2.6 The Bhidé model

Using growth models

Some of the best thinking about growth is embodied in the growth models in this chapter. Business managers may have little interest in looking back and considering how their businesses have evolved, but their models can offer insights into the problems that businesses are confronting now, and the sorts of issues that might be round the corner. Identifying a business's position on one or other of the models will provoke questions about how it is managed and directed, even if the exercise does not directly propose solutions.

The models usefully remind all managers that growth means change, and the references they make to overhauling, revolution and crisis are a reminder that change is rarely comfortable. However, even though managers worry about current and future problems, their reputations in the main rest on past successes, and so there are strong reasons for not wanting to adopt different techniques. Furthermore, a growing business is a successful business; management practice has worked so far, so why change something that does not appear to be broken? Business planning in established businesses will unsurprisingly be grounded in existing strategies. Donald Sull, a professor at

London Business School, calls this reluctance to move away from the past "active inertia".[4] Reconciling this aversion to change with the suggestion that next year's growth might well depend on management's ability to do things differently is difficult. Change asks questions therefore not just about management practice, but also about managers – whether you have the right ones. As you expand the management team you may need to recruit individuals who are very different from those currently in post. And, notwithstanding any need to expand management resources, change will probably mean that some of the current team should go.

The growth models also remind us that there is a point to some of the early stages of growth. Businesses created fully formed can suffer from missing out on the early stages of evolution. Culture and brand – the perquisites of the later stages of growth – can be manufactured, but many of the best brands and organisational cultures grow organically out of the personalities of the people who put the business together in the first place.

3   Growth enablers and drivers

THE NEXT TWO CHAPTERS consider the forces that drive and inhibit growth. This chapter addresses the question of why some businesses grow and some do not, and considers the forces that trigger and the circumstances that foster growth. It starts inside the organisation with things that are within the control of those who run it, moves on to the life cycles of products, markets and industries, and concludes with aspects of the economic and commercial environment that affect the growth of a business.

Ambition and attitude

Personal ambition has as much to do with growth as any corporate strategy or economic and commercial circumstance. Regardless of the quality of an opportunity, a business will not grow far or fast if the owners and managers do not want it to. A crucial element in any growth plan – an element that will distinguish a plan focused on growth from a standard business plan – will therefore be some consideration of the ambitions of the owners and managers.

In a 1996 *Harvard Business Review* article, "The Questions Every Entrepreneur Must Answer", Amar Bhidé argues:

> [Successful entrepreneurs] need to keep asking tough questions about where they want to go, and whether the track they're on will take them there.

Successful strategies, he says, provide clear direction, generate sufficient profits and growth, serve the enterprise in the long term and establish the right growth rate. He also encourages entrepreneurs to ask questions about their ability to execute. But above all, Bhidé encourages entrepreneurs to ask themselves what they want personally from the business and what sort of business will be required. He also encourages them to consider their appetite for risk.

If there is more than one founder or owner-manager, several sets of questions need to be asked – one for each individual. In an ideal world, owner-managers will want to work as hard as each other, will want the same things from the business, will have the same work-life priorities, will want to retire on the same day and will be happy to sell the business for the same amount of money. This, of course, is unlikely. But with discussion, negotiation and planning, different sets of personal aspirations can be reconciled with each other, and the same business can satisfy the different aspirations of different owner-managers. A crucial implication, however, is that owner-managers should attend to their personal planning as well as planning for the business, and, if there is more than one owner-manager, should maintain an open dialogue with each other. People's priorities change and plans need reviewing every so often. As the business grows, owner-managers should also consider the personal aspirations and concerns of the staff they value and wish to retain. Many founders and entrepreneurs make the mistake of assuming that newly recruited managers have the same aspirations as the founders (see Chapter 7).

Different perspectives, potential tensions

Owner-managers responsible for businesses with outside financial investors have other sets of aspirations to consider. Businesses with angel funding must acknowledge the personal ambitions of the angels. Angel funding comes in as many different forms as there are business angels. Some are happy to take relatively passive roles; others are keen to offer their experience and insight in active support of managers. Such support is not always a blessing. In extreme cases, it can seem as though angels are looking for jobs as well as investment opportunities, and run the risk of turning themselves into additional owner-managers (see Chapter 6).

Institutional sources of equity finance such as venture capitalists and private equity firms will also have their own agendas, and it is naive to assume that they will share the same goals and ambitions as the founders of the businesses in which they invest. The motivation of financiers is clear: it will be implied in the terms on which they provide finance and will involve making particular returns within specific time horizons. In many cases, institutions investing private capital in early-growth businesses anticipate the need to invest more capital in the business at a future date. In effect, they are buying an option to participate in a future funding round. This is particularly true of businesses in industries such as pharmaceuticals or businesses dependent for success on phenomena that will take time, such as changes in behaviour on the part of large groups of consumers or big corporate customers. Invariably the time horizons of venture capitalists are short, usually shorter than those of entrepreneurs. At the end of their time horizon venture capitalists are looking to make a healthy return. Their motivation is purely financial: they are in business to make money.

The motivation of entrepreneurs and owner-managers is more complicated and includes a host of personal considerations. But even at the financial level venture capitalists' and entrepreneurs' ambitions can be significantly divergent. Venture capitalists are always portfolio managers; they will invest only if they can see a reasonable chance of an investment turning into a big one. Obviously, not all their investments will turn into big ones; research shows that the majority of a venture capitalist's investments do not deliver the returns hoped for. One venture capitalist warns its potential investors that one-third of investments will fail and another third will not meet expectations. But because venture capitalists only invest in the hope of having found a big one, they are always pushing the owner-managers of their investments into decisions that improve the organisation's chances of delivering a big return, even if this also increases the risk of organisational failure.

Venture capital financing is a high-risk game in which the odds for the investor are mitigated not at the level of the organisation but at the level of the portfolio. For the venture capitalist there is always another investment. Owner-managers always think differently – even the most entrepreneurial are unlikely to have growth ambitions as aggressive as those of a venture capitalist. Owner-managers do not have the portfolio effect to mitigate their investments; for them the business is likely to be the only ball in play. It is thus inevitable that the ambitions of owner-managers and venture capitalists will be out of alignment. When negotiating a deal, financiers often push entrepreneurs and their advisers to be more aggressive and ambitious when setting targets. Venture capitalist Vinod Khosla is fond of quoting an Indian proverb:[5]

> If you shoot for the sky, you end up in the tree. If you shoot for the tree, you end up on the ground.

Tensions between financiers and founders are inevitable at the negotiation and planning stages – but these are nothing compared with the tensions that will emerge later in the organisation's history when the owner-managers are trying to achieve those targets and are increasingly aware of the implications of failure. Owner-managers in venture capital funded businesses can easily just turn into managers, and a good many end up not even being that.

For most new businesses venture capital funding is not an option. Venture capitalists fund only a small proportion of new businesses. A 2001 report for the Bank of Canada, *Venture Capital in Canada*, by Jean-Philippe Cayen, noted that in 2000 venture capital represented only 2.3% of the stock of business credit in the economy, and the situation is similar in other developed economies. Start-up businesses get even less attention from venture capitalists. A 1998 report, *Venture Capital Investment Trends in the US and Europe*, by Lawrence Rausch, indicated that seed money never accounted for more than 5% of venture capital disbursements in the United States. The combination they look for – huge growth potential, a good team, a defensible, scalable business proposition and a clear exit – is rare.

Most businesses therefore are obliged to look to their own resources, or to those of contacts, friends and family, and (if they have debt capacity) banks. But there are some entrepreneurs who choose not to take venture capital finance when they might, accepting that they will "bootstrap" their ventures instead. If entrepreneurs with venture capital are encouraged to expand their planning horizons, bootstrappers have to focus on other imperatives. "Bootstrapping clears away the clutter and makes you focus single-mindedly on the customer," says Emily Barker in an *Inc. Magazine* article about American software entrepreneur Greg Gianforte, who has built more than one business this way.[6] In Gianforte's view the rigours of being bootstrapped force the entrepreneur to focus on selling to bring cash into the business. Building a business is all about making a product that people want as fast and cheaply as possible and then selling it. Barker says:

> *I think a lot of entrepreneurs think they need money to build the business faster when they actually haven't figured out the business equation yet.*

Different approaches to funding a business are not mutually exclusive; different styles suit different stages of growth. Even Gianforte accepts that there are times in a business's life cycle when external finance is appropriate. With one of his businesses, RightNow, he looked for external finance only after the business was established and he was seeking to expand overseas. Without the money, Gianforte noted, "we would have executed the same plan, but it would have been a little slower".

For listed businesses it is very different. Shareholders who acquire their shares via a stock exchange do not have the same expectations as private equity investors, either individual or institutional, nor can they hope to have the same access to and influence over management. Managers are accountable to the board, and the board to the shareholders, but the tension between the ambitions of management and the ambitions of shareholders in a listed company is neither as pointed nor as acute as it is in private businesses funded with private equity. The ambitions of management are a more important influence on growth in a listed business than the ambitions of the owners. As Enron, Lehman Brothers, RBS (Royal Bank of Scotland) and others have shown, in listed companies the ambitions of the executive management have needed to be contained.

A must or a maybe?

Is business growth a matter of choice? Or does a business have to grow?

With big listed companies the position seems clear. Investors invest in shares in the hope that they will increase in value. CEOs of listed companies receive updates on the share price on a regular basis: during the day, after press announcements, on the way home in the car, when the market opens. Analysts assess the success of the business in terms of its performance against plan, its earnings, the credibility of its strategy and the success of management in implementing it, but ultimately what matters is the growth in its share price. Share prices are influenced by many factors, both external and internal, but they also reflect the growth of the business itself in terms of its ability to generate sustainable profit and the value of its underlying assets, intangible as well as tangible. Many directors of listed companies are under no illusion therefore that they have no alternative other than to grow their businesses.

In private businesses the position is more complicated. In the early stages of business development few would disagree with the assertion that the business has to grow or die. There is a critical mass that needs to be reached before the business can be considered to be self-sustaining. The business will need to be consistently "cash positive" (generating more cash than it is consuming). To achieve this it will need a product or service or two for which it has found a sustainable market. And it will need to be led by a team of people that is sufficiently self-sustaining to withstand the occasional resignation.

For many young businesses, however, such a state of critical mass seems curiously elusive. The experience of most who run new businesses is that their existence is fragile: just one slip could cause the whole edifice to disintegrate. Owner-managers are left with the nagging feeling that they need just another couple of products, or two or three new accounts, or another member of the management team. But when they get there they do not feel quite as secure as they thought they would feel. It is as if founding a business is not a matter of reaching a particular position but rather a continuous process of evolution.

In deciding whether or not to continue to grow a private business, once it has reached a critical mass, the personal motivation of the founders is often more important than the potential of the business. In the first version of their model of business growth, Neil Churchill and Virginia Lewis address the issue by asserting that a growing business, once it is past the existence and survival stages, needs to choose at stage 3 between success-disengagement and success-growth (see Chapter 2). Owners who choose success-disengagement are opting to step back a little and live off the fruit of their labours. They may prefer to invest in fast cars and long holidays rather than further business development. If owners choose to go for growth, their agenda and that of the business need to be aligned. Personal gain needs to be sacrificed for corporate growth.

Of course, stepping back from the business can never be at the expense of the business – otherwise the experience of enjoying the fruits of the business will be pretty short-lived. In reality, stepping back is the first stage of stepping out of the business altogether. It is not that the business no longer needs to grow, it is that the owner no longer wants or needs or is able to play a part in it. Those who talk about slowing the pace of growth are really saying that they have had enough and should get out before they do the business (their most valuable asset) serious damage. It is therefore not surprising that in later manifestations of Churchill's model (published in the *Financial Times*) the choice at stage 3 between growth and disengagement has been dropped and replaced by a stage 3 called profitability/stabilisation, which is followed by a new stage 4 called profitability/growth.

For many businesses success depends on further growth – notwithstanding any reluctance on the part of the founders. A successful architectural practice that had enjoyed spectacular growth looked for help with succession planning, including in particular how to replace its founding managing partner. There was a feeling among some of the partners that the firm had grown too big too fast, and that maybe it would benefit by shrinking closer to its previous size. This is not uncommon. Many professional partnerships hang on to management practices that suited them when they were small but no longer work when they become big. Such "small-firm-mindedness" is a typical manifestation of a yearning for the good old days. The reality, however, for a firm at this stage of its evolution is that reducing its size will not return it to the good old days. When it was young and growing with things to prove to itself and its clients, it would have been an exciting, vibrant firm where ambitious young staff could see developing futures for themselves and their colleagues. For such a firm, becoming small for the second time will be a different experience. It will have become small as a consequence of contraction; it was small the first time as a stage on the path to success. To achieve a reduction in size, staff will have to leave, and despite best efforts to the contrary it is inevitable that the best staff will choose to leave, acknowledging that the firm is no longer prepared to provide a platform for them to satisfy their ambitions. The new small firm will be a tired, jaded business, lacking in ambition. This will rub off on its clients, and before long it will find itself on a slippery downward path.

Defying the growth imperative

In many ways firms such as this have to accept that growth is an important ingredient in what makes the firm what it is; it has no alternative other than to grow. This is called "the growth imperative", and for organisations with ambition it can seem difficult to escape from its gravitational pull. One law firm is perhaps an exception that proves the rule. Founded by a group of lawyers who left one of the so-called "magic circle" firms of solicitors in London, the firm developed a niche practice in a particular area of the law. At the outset the partners decided not to increase their number; the firm would always have around half a dozen partners. If one of the partners decided to retire early the others might consider admitting another, but as a matter of strategic intent the firm was to stay the same size. This had considerable implications for management, in particular human resources management. Staff in the firm but outside the partnership knew that there were no prospects for admission to the partnership, so it was inevitable that ambitious staff would leave. Losing good staff was a matter of regret, but was felt not to present insurmountable problems in carrying on business successfully – as has proved the case. More problematic is the longer-term future of the firm.

Can it continue to thrive as the founding partners get closer towards retirement?

Small professional services firms cannot really be sold, particularly when all the partners reach retirement at the same time. When partners retire, part of the business retires with them. Big firms get round this by creating a self-renewing wheel in which good staff coming through the firm buy into the partnership and in effect fund the retirement of their seniors. In the above example this could not happen. To some extent the decision to defy the growth imperative curtailed the life of the firm. In some businesses a decision not to grow need not have such dire consequences, but it is difficult to maintain standards, recruit and retain good staff, and satisfy clients and customers who are prepared to pay good money if a business chooses not to grow.

Positively countering the negative

Instead of going for the no-growth option, businesses worried about the negative effects of growth might do better to address those that cause them most concern. This may be to do with ensuring that:

- the business remains enjoyable to manage as it grows. Much that makes a small business special is happenstance, often depending on personality, good and bad fortune. In a bigger business, even the informal and the accidental need to be formalised, but particular characteristics and qualities of an organisation's culture and style can be preserved and managed as it gets bigger (see Chapter 7);

- the management infrastructure keeps pace with growth and does not end up constrained by using techniques that worked when it was smaller, but not now that it is larger;

- enough attention and resources go into internal communication. These matters look after themselves in a small business, when people see each other every day. In a bigger business, management needs to work on them.

Managing the negative implications of growth can help strengthen the platform for the next stage of growth.

New products and services

Crucial to growth is how successfully a company responds to the changing needs of customers for products and services. But the important ability to identify and respond to the changing demands of customers is not reliant solely on rational planning processes. As George Bernard Shaw observes in *Man and Superman*:

> *The reasonable man adapts himself to the world; the unreasonable one persists in trying to adapt the world to himself. Therefore all progress depends on the unreasonable man.*

Discover the need, identify the opportunity

Responding to customer needs requires distinguishing what customers really want from what they say they want, and intuiting what they do not yet know they want. As Anthony Ulwick, a consultant and innovation expert, argued in a 2002 *Harvard Business Review* article, "Turn Customer Input into Innovation", customer feedback is used properly when it is used to identify what customers value rather than what they say they want. Conversely, the slogan adopted by Ford some years ago – "everything we do is driven by you" – was indeed meant to suggest a product portfolio designed in response to a careful analysis of consumer needs. But many thought that portfolio was dull. Customers want to be surprised, and they will not be surprised if businesses ask them what they want and just give it to them. Customers are not the best people to imagine what they might want, beyond specific changes to products. So be careful when giving customers what they say they want.

When identifying and imagining customer needs it is important not to confuse what the market needs with what you want to supply. Too many entrepreneurs expect customers to be as enthusiastic about their ideas as they are. There is a world of difference between an opportunity and a good idea or a "nice piece of kit". John Steinbeck captures the issue nicely in an exchange between Adam and Will in his novel *East of Eden*:

> *"I come from a whole goddam family of inventors," said Will. "We had ideas for breakfast. We had ideas instead of breakfast. We had*

so many ideas we forgot to make the money for groceries ... I'm the only one in the family, except my mother, who didn't have ideas, and I'm the only one who ever made a dime."

Managers interested in sustainable growth should note the following distinctions between ideas and opportunities:

- Good ideas are timeless and priceless, but good opportunities are defined by more pragmatic qualities. An opportunity is time-specific: it is tied to a particular time and set of circumstances. It is not priceless either: it has a value, and its value is associated with the right time and place. In the world of business, times and circumstances change and opportunities therefore expire. It might be difficult to measure the value of an opportunity in advance, but because the value is tied to its time and circumstance it too is transient. If an opportunity is not pinned down at the right time it will not be worth anything. Good ideas can come too early, before the market is ready for them. The idea Adam was getting excited about in *East of Eden* was to refrigerate lettuces and ship them from California to New York in the winter. He invested a lot of his own money in the idea. The problem was that he attempted to implement it before the first world war; customers would not be accustomed to lettuces in February, Adam's critic, Will, argued. In any case the transport infrastructure was inadequate and the lettuces were rotten when they arrived. But no one today would consider Adam's idea daft. An idea can also come too late, when a company with a competing (and sometimes inferior) idea may have already grasped the opportunity and built a defensible market position. Success can come from taking advantage of the zeitgeist, but the spirit of the times changes. The time has to be right not just for the market but also for the entrepreneur and for whoever is providing the money.

- Opportunities, compared with ideas, are related to specific market circumstances, particularly customer and client needs. There is often no reason why the market should ever find a need for your idea, no matter how brilliant it is. As if to prove the point some entrepreneurs start not with an idea at all, but with an attempt to identify and isolate a market need. A market need can be quantified and valued. Only after the need has been defined will such entrepreneurs turn their attention to generating the solution, scouring the universities or the design agencies for someone who can come up with a product or service to address the need. Good opportunities are therefore intimately related to customer needs.

■ Ideas are abstractions; opportunities are grounded in reality. Opportunities respond far more to hard work than to inspiration. Understanding the distinction between a good opportunity and a good idea is crucial for managers looking for new ways to grow.

■ Unlike an idea, an opportunity, in and of itself, is not unique. Uniqueness is created when a team of individuals with a particular blend of experience and expertise successfully takes advantage of an opportunity and turns it into a difficult-to-replicate business.

Execution is all

Just as businesses are built on opportunities not ideas, so successful growth is a matter of execution rather than invention. Inventors are people who dream things up. Entrepreneurs are people who turn dreams into reality. Invention is about creativity and imagination; these qualities are useful for entrepreneurs, but entrepreneurship is far more about implementation. Inventors wrestle with ideas; entrepreneurs convert ideas into businesses. In a study of entrepreneurship conducted between 1982 and 1989 in the United States, only 12% of founders attributed the success of their companies to "an unusual or extraordinary idea"; but some 88% attributed their success to "exceptional execution of an ordinary idea".[7] There are some individuals who have managed to combine both sets of skills, such as James Dyson, inventor of, among other things, the dual cyclone bagless vacuum cleaner. But Dyson is an exception to the rule. Trevor Baylis, inventor of the wind-up radio, is often cited as another, though it was only after an episode of the BBC's *Tomorrow's*

World in 1994 and Baylis's subsequent association with accountant Christopher Staines and South African entrepreneur Rory Stear that the invention started on the path to commercial realisation. Even Bill Gates, who is much more in the Dyson than the Baylis mould, relied in the early days on Steve Ballmer, Microsoft's 30th employee and first business manager.

Crazy ideas people are often able to grow a business only when more down-to-earth and pragmatic people work with them. For many inventors growth happens only after they have walked away. W.H. Hoover knew nothing about hoovers. Several peoples on both sides of the Atlantic had developed good ideas for using suction to remove dust and debris, and numerous patents had been filed. In 1901 H. Cecil Booth patented a motorised vacuum cleaner. He started the British Vacuum Cleaner Company and his industrial cleaners, powered first by steam and then by oil, were pulled from site to site by horse. Hoover was in the leather harness business, but he had problems as the car quickly began to take over from the horse and cart. It was his wife's cousin, James Murray Spangler, who had thought long and hard about vacuum cleaner technology and had added the all-important brushes to the machine, which was then patented. Spangler did not know how to commercialise the idea, and thought he could not afford to, so he sold the idea and the patents to Hoover. Hoover's Electric Suction Sweeper Company first started selling the Hoover "Model O" in 1908 for the princely sum of $60. Early adopters were enthusiastic, and Hoover became rich. His success was triggered by a structural recession in the industry he knew best, and fostered by his powers of execution in an industry he did not know at all.

For most it means recognising that the inventor or the ideas person cannot go it alone. Some ideas people and entrepreneurs remain in touch with their ideas by building up teams of people who know how to commercialise the ideas, and how to execute. Businesses often stand a better chance of getting off the ground in the first place, and grow further and faster, if they are put together by teams of individuals with complementary skills (see Chapter 7).

Stars, dogs and the product life cycle

Markets for products and services mature, and businesses ambitious for growth need to be aware of the changes that maturity brings. Customers for a new product behave very differently from customers for a mature product.

One of the best-known frameworks for analysing the life cycle of products and services is the matrix devised by the Boston Consulting Group, usually known as the BCG matrix (see Figure 3.1).

The framework introduced into the vocabulary of managers the terms cash cow, dog, star and problem child. Many product and service portfolio analyses have attempted to categorise products and services using the matrix. The labels in some ways are unfortunate; many managers have assumed that they should be responsible for "stars". But as Figure 3.1 shows, stars are products that have lots of potential in terms of market growth and current market share – but it is only potential; in a rapidly growing market there is a lot of uncertainty requiring significant investment. The products that generate cash for the business are older and more established; no longer in a growing market, cash cows benefit nonetheless from high market share and require relatively little expenditure to maintain that position. Stars have potential, but they are risky; cash cows are generating cash now. At least stars are generating revenue. Problem children have low market share in markets with high potential; they are consuming resources but not generating returns. Will they ever? Managers need to consider whether it is worth maintaining the investment in the hope that problem children will turn into stars and then cash cows. The risk is that they might turn into dogs: products achieving low market share in low-growth markets, demanding little investment but generating little return.

The BCG matrix is much used, but it has shortcomings. There are perils associated with focusing too much on markets that are growing, while shrinking markets can offer opportunities for businesses ambitious for growth. Market share is not the only thing that matters and is as much a function of the size of a business as it is a reflection of the success of its strategy. Small businesses entering established markets will never have significant market share, but that does not

Star		**Problem child**	
Revenue	+ + +	Revenue	+
Expenditure	– – –	Expenditure	– – –
Cash flow	neutral	Cash flow	– –
Cash cow		**Dog**	
Revenue	+ + + +	Revenue	+
Expenditure	– –	Expenditure	–
Cash flow	+ +	Cash flow	neutral

Market growth (vertical axis: High to Low)

Market share (horizontal axis: High)

Source: After Boston Consulting Group

FIG 3.1 The BCG matrix

mean they cannot be successful businesses. In general, the BCG analysis generates the most insight for businesses that are big already. As with many frameworks, this one works less well when applied to younger, smaller businesses.

Geoffrey Moore has another take on new products and the way they and the markets for them evolve in his book *Crossing the Chasm*.[8] His chief interest is the market for high-technology products, but his observations shed light on how to market any new product or service.

Building on the earlier work of sociologist Everett Rogers, Moore writes most interestingly about the "chasm", the gulf between the geeky enthusiasts that he, following Rogers, calls "early adopters" and the mainstream of the market (see Figure 3.2). A new company providing a new product may find it relatively easy to excite some early adopters, who might be prepared to pay a lot for an as yet unproven and unreliable product. But early adopters are always likely to be few in number, and their attitudes and enthusiasms are rarely typical of the market as a whole. The mainstream is often a lot more difficult to persuade. An ambitious company in a new market with a new product will have to find ways of crossing the chasm or its growth ambitions will not be satisfied. The mainstream will be more

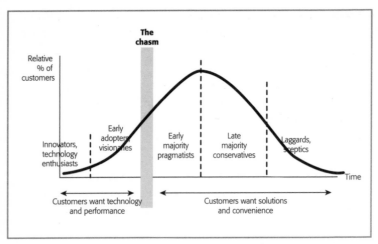

The chasm

Relative % of customers

Innovators, technology enthusiasts

Early adopters visionaries

Early majority pragmatists

Late majority conservatives

Laggards, sceptics

Time

Customers want technology and performance

Customers want solutions and convenience

Source: Geoffrey Moore, *Crossing the Chasm*, Harper Business, 1991

FIG 3.2 Crossing the chasm

price-conscious and more interested in utility than in novelty and technology. In parallel with the change in customer perceptions will be a change in the competitive environment, with new and larger competitors entering the market to drive down price and improve quality and reliability. A business ambitious for growth will have to change its marketing strategy if it wants to capture mainstream customers. It will also have to look long and hard at its operating model for efficiencies if it is to maintain its margins under pressure from new competition.

Focus versus diversification

Crucial to business success and growth is being able to recognise and capitalise on your competitive advantage. When doing this a business ambitious for growth may look for opportunities not just with its current portfolio of products and within its current customer and client relationships. In considering diversification it needs to think carefully about the competitive advantage that has delivered growth to date. Either single-focus or diversification-based strategies can provide platforms for growth, and both have their champions:

- **Focus.** A company sticks to what it knows best, thus giving itself the best chance of developing an expertise that can be defended against other market entrants. Focus enthusiasts argue that any attempt to widen a company's range of activities runs the risk of diluting its competitive advantage and spreading its resources too thin. In other words, it is better to do something really well than a variety of things not very well.

- **Diversification.** A company ambitious for growth adds different products and services to its portfolio because it is only by broadening its range that it will extend its reach and increase its size. Furthermore, it is simply too risky to have all your eggs in one basket. Diversification enthusiasts argue that well-diversified product, service and customer portfolios are inherently less risky and more sustainable than businesses with a narrow focus.

Supporters of the focus line often argue that core competence should be the cornerstone of an effective strategy. But C.K. Prahalad and Gary Hamel, who came up with the concept in their 1990 *Harvard Business Review* article, "The Core Competence of the Organisation", did not argue in favour of a single core competence but rather a plurality of core competencies around which a strategy, product or service and organisation is built.

More aligned with focus as a keystone of growth is the thinking of Chris Zook, an American academic, in *Profit from the Core.*[9] Basing their ten-year study on more than 2,000 technology, service and product companies in a variety of industries, Zook and his co-author, James Allen, argue that most growth strategies fail to deliver value – and even destroy it – primarily because they diversify inappropriately from their core business. Zook and Allen argue that three factors differentiate businesses with growth strategies that succeed from those that fail:

- they achieve full potential in their core business;
- they recognise that successful expansion has to be into logical adjacent businesses surrounding that core;
- they acknowledge that their core will need to continuously evolve in response to market turbulence and changes of circumstance.

Zook and Allen draw attention to some telling paradoxes at the heart of many growth stories:

It is almost as if most growth strategies harbour a dark, destructive force that causes companies to reduce their focus on their core business and thereby to depart from the basis of their real differentiation.

Entrepreneurs who have founded a successful business too often believe that they can walk on water and repeat the trick. So-called "serial entrepreneurs" are often people who have been lucky enough to make their money on a venture and then spend the rest of their careers spending it on other less successful ventures. Being "entrepreneurial" in many big businesses is a matter of rushing around after the next new thing rather than applying an entrepreneurial mindset to the part of the enterprise responsible for its success in the first place. As Zook and Allen say:

The better performing of your businesses units are likely to be those operating the furthest below their full potential.

Why? Because those parts of your business that performed well in the past have provided management with an excuse for not paying them the attention that would ensure they perform even better in the present and future. It is only too tempting for managers not to invest in the business they understand the best. However, Zook and Allen add:

The stronger your core business, the more opportunities you have both to move into profitable adjacencies and to lose focus.

A strong core provides the resources but is also an excuse for management to explore other initiatives, at the expense of attending to the heart of the business. For the perils of one manifestation of the temptation to expand at the expense of your core – mergers and acquisitions – see Chapter 8.

Zook and Allen concede that, although the core is important, growth will eventually depend on moves beyond it. In a later book, *Beyond the Core*, Zook makes the case for successful diversification

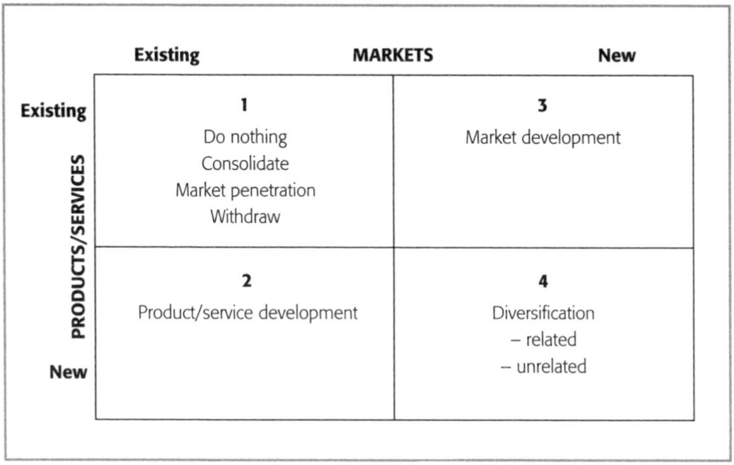

	Existing	MARKETS	New
Existing	**1** Do nothing Consolidate Market penetration Withdraw		**3** Market development
New	**2** Product/service development		**4** Diversification – related – unrelated

(left axis label: **PRODUCTS/SERVICES**)

Source: Based on Ansoff, I, "Strategies for Diversification", *Harvard Business Review,* 1957

FIG 3.3 Igor Ansoff's two-by-two matrix

rather than no diversification at all, while arguing that the further you step away from the reasons for your success the riskier it will be.[10]

Many others have written about the risks of diversification. Igor Ansoff's two-by-two matrix (a version of which is illustrated in Figure 3.3) features in many business plans focusing on growing the top line.[11] Box 2 is about finding new products to take to existing markets, while box 3 is about finding new markets for existing products. Both these strategies are inherently riskier than trying to increase penetration in existing markets with the current product portfolio, though as a growth strategy this will be constrained by the size and growth potential of the overall market. Both 3 and 2 are less risky than a diversification strategy (box 4): seeking to develop new products for entirely new markets, where the risks are compounded. But both 3 and 2 are also, in the long term at least, inherently less risky than the version of box 1 that involves doing nothing at all and watching the competitive environment evolve around you.

Of course, a business that is already successfully diversified can take advantage of the portfolio effect to mitigate its risks, and play in all four of Ansoff's boxes, with different products or businesses in each one.

Intangibles: intellectual property and brand

As noted earlier, a successful business that has satisfied a market opportunity with a product or service and that is successfully winning profitable new business will find itself attracting the attention of powerful competition. An important way for a business to defend what it has achieved, and to provide a platform for further growth, is through the effective management of its intangible assets.

In some industries, intellectual property – patents, copyrights and trademarks – is critical. Big companies in the pharmaceutical industry can justify their enormous research and development expenditure only because they know they can protect the pharmacological compounds they develop from copycats for a significant period of time. Intellectual property is also an important element in other high-tech industries.

Many businesses invest too much time and effort in protecting their intellectual property. A patent has real value only if the company owning it is prepared to spend money defending it. Defending patents is an expensive business – even more expensive than obtaining one in the first place – and is often beyond the means of many smaller businesses. As well as high-tech firms, big, wealthy companies with deep pockets play the patent game and, as Figure 3.4 suggests, invest a lot of time (and money) in suing and defending themselves against lawsuits. Again, a patent is only worth obtaining and fighting for if there is a good chance it will secure commercial advantage and value for a significant period of time. In many industries the next, superior product is only just around the corner, and it may use an alternative mechanism or formula or programme that will enable its owner to sidestep the patent you have spent so much time and money on – resources that might have been better spent on marketing or product development.

Some companies, however, argue that time and money spent on patents is time and money spent on marketing. They invest in patents not because of the property rights they bring but because they help reinforce their owners' credibility as cutting-edge players in the industry. For such companies the management of intellectual property has become an element of brand management.

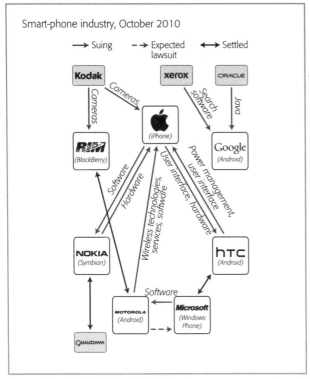

Source: Bristol York; company reports; *The Economist*

FIG 3.4 Who's suing whom

Brand is another intangible asset, the development of which can help defend a hard-won market position and provide a platform for further growth. A brand is not just the name and logo protected by law and called a trademark. A brand is the indefinable essence or promise of a product or service, comprising many elements and characteristics of the product and the business that produced it. Because a brand is difficult to define, it can be more difficult to copy than the product or service itself.

Chapter 7 considers the role other intangible elements – culture and values – play in the management of the growing business.

Markets and industries

When planning for growth it is important to understand the dynamics of both the industry (the collection of producers and suppliers making and supplying similar products and services) and the market (the collection of customers interested in an industry's products or services) a business operates in. When understanding the industry a company needs to consider its competition; when understanding its market a company needs to understand its customers.

Life cycles

Industries and markets, like companies, have life cycles. A new industry will be dominated by entrepreneurs looking not just to shape their businesses but also to dominate the industry, to define its standards and protocols, and in some instances to become the industry – for years a vacuum cleaner was a Hoover, for example. Younger markets and industries tend to be shaped by smaller, entrepreneurial companies rather than bigger companies. Smaller businesses are better at taking advantage of the uncertainty that is inherent in a new market than big businesses, which in turn are far better at allocating resources to the well-defined opportunities that are more likely to characterise mature markets.

Part of the allure of a new market is the myth of first-mover advantage. If you can be there at the start, what is to stop you getting big within the industry that develops to serve the market? Quite a lot, actually. Firms like Hoover are the exceptions that prove the rule that most new businesses do not turn into big ones just as a consequence of inventing an industry and then sticking with it. New businesses that invent industries attract competition. Many small businesses argue that they do not have competition when what they really mean is that the competition has not yet discovered them or the opportunity. When the competition does arrive it is likely to be better resourced than the small businesses that have successfully identified and developed the opportunity.

Title Research, a company specialising in probate research, virtually invented online genealogy for amateurs in the UK when it launched findmypast.co.uk, putting birth, marriage and death records online and charging customers to access them. The website generated more profit in its first year of trading than the company that founded it did in that same year. But to sustain momentum Title Research needed to invest in more data sets, such as census records. It was only once Title Research had validated the market in the UK that an established American player, ancestry.com, appeared, equipped with census records ready to launch, and offering birth, marriage and death records to customers for free. Findmypast.co.uk went overnight from being a success to being a business under siege with a precarious future. Within two years Title Research had sold it. This is not an unusual story. Big businesses often leave the opening up of new industries to small upstarts, preferring to step in only when the potential has been confirmed. Thus smaller businesses rarely turn into big businesses as an industry matures, but rather are replaced by them.

Most importantly, as the Title Research example illustrates, a company seeking to grow needs to understand not just its current competitors and customers, but also its next competitors and customers.

Opportunities of size

Big businesses and small businesses do coexist in the same industry, and the symbiotic nature of their relationship can provide other routes to growth – certainly for the smaller industry players. When times are good, money is plentiful, the economy is growing and chief executives are congratulating themselves for growing with it, big business is out with its chequebook. In economically sunny 1999, with the markets fuelled by the start of the dotcom boom and work generated by the millennium bug, Ford Motor Company wrote a cheque for just over £1 billion ($1.65 billion) for UK auto-spares business Kwik-Fit, paying a 33% premium over the market price for the business. Kwik-Fit's founding entrepreneur, Sir Tom Farmer, made £75m ($124m) from selling his 8% share in the business, and took a senior role at Ford. Ford's president and chief executive officer, Jacques Nasser, was reported by BBC news as saying:

[The acquisition] is an important step towards Ford's goal to become the world's leading consumer company that provides automotive products and services through world class brands.

Less than three years later the economic environment was much shakier following the bursting of the dotcom bubble. Kwik-Fit was back on the market. Ford's new boss, keen to roll out a new strategy in difficult times, sold it in August 2002 for £330m ($545m), less than one-third of the price paid for the business back in 1999. A Ford spokesman was reported by BBC news as having observed:

The sale of Kwik-Fit is a positive outcome for Ford. As we have said since the beginning of the year, we want to divest non-core assets and this gets us very close towards our goal for the year.

Had Ford paid too much for Kwik-Fit in 1999? Had it sold the business too cheaply in 2002? These are the wrong questions to ask. What is more interesting is that an entrepreneur did well in getting a good price when selling the company in 1999, and a private equity firm, CVC Capital Partners, did well in buying it below value in 2002. The wheels of big business move at a different speed and often in a different direction from the nimble feet of the entrepreneurially minded. Entrepreneurs need to remember this, particularly when the business news, which is almost always dominated by noise from big business, is full of doom and gloom.

Another example is that of Lloyd Dorfman, the founder of Travelex, a foreign-exchange business, who recalled that at the launch of the euro on January 1st 2002 many people thought he "should have been in mourning" at the elimination of most of Europe's national currencies. He looked at it differently. The introduction of the euro certainly accelerated the exit from the industry of banks and other large competitors, several of which sold their foreign-exchange businesses to Travelex. However, in the longer term, the market would benefit from an increase in international travel and cross-border trade. Market contraction in the short term gave Travelex the opportunity to consolidate so that it could take advantage of long-term exponential growth.

Assessing the forces at work

A common way of analysing an industry is through the five forces outlined by Michael Porter in his book *Competitive Strategy*.[12] Five-forces analysis attempts to assess the health of the competitive environment in an industry. A company can then consider its own strategy in the context of the industry in which it operates. The five forces are as follows:

- The threat of substitute products and the ability of customers to switch to them.

- The threat posed by new entrants to the industry – and the extent to which there are barriers to entry.

- The power of customers – their ability to dictate terms to you. If there are relatively few customers for your product, each customer will have more power.

- The power of suppliers – their ability to dictate terms to you. Again, a monopolistic supplier will be able to dictate price and influence quality.

- Competitive rivalry between industry players.

A company can consider the strength of the forces in its particular industry and the extent to which the forces are favourable or unfavourable before assessing its response.

An analysis of the industry using five-forces analysis is just a start. Companies planning for growth need to understand how their competitors operate individually. They also need to understand how the industry might change, particularly how competitors are likely to respond to any initiatives included within the growth plan.

Understanding the complexities

It is easy sometimes to oversimplify the business environment. A company has suppliers and customers with whom it strikes up a relationship. It also has competitors on which it keeps a wary eye, but which by and large it sees as the enemy. Analytical tools such as Porter's five forces can encourage businesses to think simplistically about their competitive environments. But the biggest opportunities are available only to those able to think the thoughts that others do not think. Everyone doing five-forces analysis on the same industry will come to similar conclusions. Businesses serious about growth need to think differently. They should start by understanding the subtleties that exist even in the simplest of industries and markets.

In agency businesses, such as estate agents and recruitment agents, customers and suppliers can get confused. A house seller "supplies" the product that an estate agent sells. But it is the house seller who pays the estate agent's fee, not the customer who looks at the estate agent's inventory in its shop window. In a recruitment agency, it is the business doing the recruiting that pays the agency's fee, but the relationship between the agency and the person being placed has many of the characteristics of the company-customer relationship. In complicated markets the definitions of other market players can change. Competitors can turn into collaborators as well as, on some occasions, customers.

Some writers have turned to distant frames of reference when trying to identify and explain subtleties not just in complicated markets and industries, but in simple ones too. Drawing on mathematics' game theory, American academics Adam Brandenburger and Barry Nalebuff conceive of the market as a place where "complementors" as well as competitors, customers and suppliers do business. Complementors, who can operate on the supply side or the customer side, are market participants whose existence improves the position of another company without necessarily being a customer or a supplier. A player is your supply-side complementor if it is more attractive for a supplier to provide you with resources when it is also supplying the other player than when supplying you alone. Conversely, a player is your supply-side competitor if it is less attractive for a supplier to provide you with resources when it is also supplying the other player than when it is supplying you alone. A player is your customer-side complementor if customers value your product more when they have the other player's product than when they have your product alone. Conversely, a player is your customer-side competitor if customers value your product less when they have the other player's product than when they have your product alone.

For example, video renters and retailers and cinemas were initially seen as competitors, but they found they had a complementary relationship – they could work to each other's mutual advantage. Similarly, independent component manufacturers in, for example, the car industry, who are accustomed to outsourcing significant elements of the manufacturing process, find themselves in complementary relationships, not just with the car manufacturer but with each other. Again, understanding the nuances of the market, the motives of the players and the rules of the game will help a business identify fresh opportunities and grow faster.

Expanding horizons

Sooner or later a company ambitious for growth, as well as looking to new products and new customers, will look for new business internationally. Companies in small economies will feel the temptation sooner than those in big ones. The United States has an economy big enough to satisfy the growth aspirations of many ambitious local companies until they become very large. Conversely, companies in the UK and the Netherlands, for example, have had to turn to overseas markets to satisfy their growth ambitions much earlier in their evolution.

Many companies' first moves overseas are at the request of customers who are happy with a supplier's services in one country and want to use them in another. This helps reduce some of the risks inherent in international expansion, but even so new types of risks will need to be mastered for such expansion to prove an effective growth enabler. These include control risk in a business operation that is likely to be geographically distant, and management risk in understanding cultural differences, which will affect both how the business is to be run internally and how the industry and market in which it hopes to operate work.

These risks are often underestimated, particularly by companies that have experienced success only in their domestic markets and often assume that what works at home will also work abroad. The United States is a famous graveyard for the ambitions of British companies seeking to expand overseas; and Western companies have too often presumed the Chinese would welcome them with open arms and learn how to do things properly, only to find themselves taken advantage of by canny and ruthless new partners and competitors. Some important considerations are as follows:

- **Local market differences.** Markets behave very differently in different countries at both the macro and micro levels. Routes to market are therefore different. Big supermarket chains dominate the UK groceries market in a way that is not seen in euro-zone countries. Once a route to market has been agreed, a company must understand that customers and clients in other countries behave differently and have different expectations. "We've had mayonnaise issues," noted Andrew Rolfe, then CEO of UK sandwich chain Pret a Manger, when opening in New York. "Mayonnaise is quite popular in Britain, but Americans aren't so receptive." Pret a Manger experimented with "drier" sandwiches with some success, though the egg Florentine that replaced the egg mayonnaise was described by one critic as having the "colour of neon".

- **Local industry differences.** There will be different competitors in different countries. Industries will be structured differently, so a company's competitive advantage might well differ from country to country. Supply chain issues will need serious consideration. Can you take advantage of and extend existing supply chains to your new overseas businesses? Or will the cost of exporting dictate the need to source materials and conduct assembly, manufacturing or service delivery remotely? What are the control implications?

- **People management.** This is the issue most likely to be underestimated. Employment and regulation regimes differ significantly from one country to another, with implications for recruitment, performance management, training, health and safety and redundancy. It is highly unlikely that staff management systems can be imported from head office to a new overseas subsidiary. Cultural differences will also need to be accounted for: different attitudes to authority and control, the work ethic, customer service. A crucial issue when expanding overseas is the appointment of senior managers. Should a company recruit local people or send over expatriates?

Expatriates will understand the company best and are more likely to be trusted by headquarters, but locals will understand the local industry and market.

■ **Entry strategy.** This will need careful thought, particularly with regard to how it affects organisational structure. In some countries companies must have a local "partner"; but even when this is not a legal requirement, most companies attempt to minimise the risks through some form of local tie-up, perhaps a joint venture with a local company. Franchising (see Chapter 7) is a common route to international expansion. A local presence helps reinforce credibility as well as secure local knowledge. When Owlstone, a high-tech gas-sensor business originally spun out of Cambridge University by its founders, sought to exploit opportunities with the American military, it decided to establish a new American company, Owlstone Inc, which took ownership of the original UK company. Only by having formal and legal ownership established in the United States did Owlstone believe it could secure the contracts it was after.

The economic environment

Generally it is easier to grow a business when the economic environment is favourable. Money for investment is more easily obtained; customers and clients are more inclined to increase orders. Conversely, once a recession is established, planning assumptions in big companies are changed: budgets for the next year are reduced, discretionary expenditure is cut, acquisitions are postponed, recruitment is frozen and staff numbers are cut. Actions such as these by firms that dominate their markets and industries in turn fuel the economic malaise they were intended to address. Small businesses, particularly those further down the supply chain, feel the consequences of these actions, with order books cut. As small businesses generally have more restricted portfolios of products and services than big businesses, and often depend on one or two large accounts, a 1–2% cut by a big company can mean a 20–30% reduction in the turnover of a small one. This could be the difference between life and death, unless the small company finds new business or adapts fast.

One company specialising in furniture design and installation is an example. During the most recent economic boom the company, which had previously focused on academic, ecclesiastical and other institutions with historically valuable buildings and spaces, expanded its portfolio of services and product lines and began to sell to blue-chip companies that were refitting their corporate headquarters. By 2008, the corporate sector accounted for almost 40% of the company's business, with RBS being its largest client that year. By 2009, the corporate business had evaporated and the company had to embark on a programme of redundancies and other cost-cutting measures in order to survive.

Business planning cycles and economic cycles are rarely aligned. Business planning cycles in big businesses in particular turn slowly: one cycle can take six months; more strategy meetings and more planning meetings are needed before things change significantly again. It is not surprising that big businesses often fall into recessions late, and that they are slow to acknowledge the new dawn. And big companies, particularly ones that spend time benchmarking their performance against their competitors, often behave like sheep, seeking to cut at the same time. They are thus less likely to make the most of the opportunities presented by recessions. Smaller companies, though more likely to be damaged by a recession, can often respond to an upturn more quickly.

Boom-time warning signs

The growth generated when times are good can prove to be illusory and not sustainable. Business leaders determined to establish robust, sustainable growth should watch out for the symptoms of false, boom-time growth:

■ **Unsustainable growth in asset values.** In particular investments: in recent booms it has been houses, commercial property, stocks and shares; before house ownership was common and before stockmarkets were sophisticated, it was grain, or tulips. The subsequent collapse of every market has always given the lie to the permanence of the growth in values.

Business owners need to distinguish between the growth in reported value and real growth in business.

■ **Deluded thinking.** Former British prime minister Gordon Brown will never be allowed to forget his claim that he had put an end to boom and bust. Brown is not alone. Herbert Hoover, when accepting the nomination of the Republican Party in 1928, proclaimed:

> We in America today are nearer to the final triumph over poverty than ever before in the history of any land ... We have not yet reached the goal, but given a chance to go forward with the policies of the last eight years, we shall soon, with the help of God, be in sight of the day when poverty will be banished from this nation.

Most of the electorate agreed with Hoover, and he won a landslide victory in the presidential election. In 1929 Wall Street crashed, heralding the biggest recession of the century.

■ **People and companies take silly risks.** The rise in asset values characteristic of boom economies is fuelled in part by investors and businesses taking risky decisions, and then competing with each other for the right to participate in even dafter decisions. To stoke the fire further, money is borrowed to fund flaky strategies. But asset values go down as well as up. Debt remains constant even if the cost of paying interest on it may not, and when the boom is over and asset values have plummeted what is owed may far exceed the value of what is owned.

■ **Business plans are increasingly unrealistic.** When money is easy and cheap to obtain, business plans become increasingly unrealistic, and when a boom is rolling reasons are found to sidestep robust planning disciplines designed to protect businesses from folly. In the boom years running up to 2008, and in the earlier dotcom boom, many business plans were based on the flimsiest of assumptions. At the heart of many were projections of infinitely increasing returns, long before the putative business had generated any cash flow. There was much talk of a "new paradigm" and so investors had to find new criteria on which to justify their investments. Measures derived from profit and cash flow became less important than market share or subjective assessments of future advances in technology or the size of the market. As Chapter 5 makes clear, healthy growth is all about the quality of cash flow.

■ **Never-ending faith.** Those who say that what goes up must come down are too easily dismissed as doom-mongers when times are good. Even those who are prepared to admit the inevitability of the end of the boom are likely to call it a "correction" or choose to believe that any slowdown will be gradual and therefore manageable. People do not want the boom to end; it cannot for the simple reason that they depend on it not ending. Even when the numbers begin to turn bad there is a tendency to remain bullish. Red numbers look black through rose-tinted spectacles. The consequence is that the bust is a nasty surprise and the bigger the boom, the nastier the bust.

■ **Growth hides weaknesses.** When times are good the flaws in business models and strategies lie hidden, ready to strike when times turn bad. Growth in good times hides operational strategic flaws; it does not eliminate them.

Entrepreneurs born in adversity

Recessions are cradles of entrepreneurship. Many entrepreneurs are neither born nor bred, they are created by force of circumstance. Many small businesses are born when their founders' long-standing employers "let them go". The redundancy payments that sweeten the pill have in many instances provided the working capital for the new businesses that have been founded as a result. Most of these new entrepreneurs would not have taken the decision on their own. In a report for the Kauffman Foundation, Dane Stangler argues:[13]

> Good things do grow out of recessions. Hundreds of thousands of individuals do not wait for others to ease their economic pain – they create jobs for themselves and others.

And those who find themselves jobless when recession hits should heed the advice of Declan Donnellan, a theatre director and writer: "Take your work seriously, but improvise your career."[14]

The sharper the recession the greater the source of opportunity and the longer the list of businesses that are created; indeed, according to a study sponsored by the Kauffman Foundation, well over half of Fortune 500 and almost half of the fastest-growing firms in the United States were founded in a recession or a bear market:[15]

> *Each year new firms steadily recreate the economy, generating jobs and innovations. These companies may be invisible, or they may one day grow into household names. But they constantly come into being as individuals bring forth their economic futures.*

In a 2003 article in the *American Economic Review* Alexander Field argued that the 1930s was the most "technologically progressive" decade of the 20th century. FedEx began operations in April 1973 in the depths of a recession. Its original name, Federal Express, was a sly swipe at the Federal Reserve, with which its founder, Frederick W. Smith, had hoped to get a contract. He did not succeed, but the company that delivered 186 packages to 25 cities on its first night of operations was by 2008 managing more than 7.5m shipments a day worldwide. General Electric (GE) was founded in 1876 by Thomas Edison, creator of the electric light bulb, in the severe depression following the financial crisis known as the Panic of 1873. Hewlett-Packard Development Company was born in a Palo Alto garage in 1939, towards the end of the Great Depression, supported by an initial investment of $538.

Businesses founded in recessions seem to be better placed for growth when times turn more benign. A 2009 study for Cambridge University's Institute for Manufacturing, *The Cambridge high tech cluster*, by Alex Drofiak and Elizabeth Garnsey, suggested that high-tech firms were more successful if started in tough times; indeed, high-tech businesses founded in Cambridge in the 1990s recession enjoyed consistently better survival rates than those started in the boom years that followed.

Many of today's big businesses were yesterday's start-ups in recessions long since forgotten. Entrepreneurs have always been peculiarly suited to difficult economic circumstances. William Sahlman, a professor at Harvard Business School, defined entrepreneurship as "the relentless pursuit of opportunity without regard to tangible resources currently controlled" and "the continuous development of intangible resources to pursue opportunity". In other words: "I haven't got the money, the people or indeed any other of the things you might expect of someone looking to put together a new business – but I'm determined to do it anyway." It seems that adversity, whether caused by personal circumstances or the commercial environment, is almost a precondition of entrepreneurship. As Victor Kiam, an American entrepreneur and investor, observed:

> *Entrepreneurs are simply those who understand that there is little difference between obstacle and opportunity and are able to turn both to their advantage.*

Now transformed into today's big businesses, yesterday's entrepreneurial businesses will no longer be able to take advantage of the full range of opportunities on offer.

Recessionary opportunities

There are undoubtedly some types of opportunities that are more likely than others to turn into growing businesses when times are bad. In general, in bad times people continue to buy food. It is easy to assume that the demand for luxury goods is more likely to suffer, but the purchasing power of the super-rich is relatively unaffected by recessions, though people may decide to be less conspicuous in their consumption. Some corners of the market for ultra exclusive products seem to be fairly recession proof. While most car manufacturers were reporting year-on-year sales decreases, in autumn 2008 Rolls-Royce was reporting that it was still on track to beat forecast.

Business managers looking for opportunities when times are bad need to look a lot more carefully at market microclimates. Consumers on fixed incomes – pensioners, for example – are under less pressure than others to change habits; such consumers are more likely to be affected by inflation and the interest they are earning on their savings. For most parents, it will always be a case of "children first" regardless of the economy.

Consumers are only too often prepared to act irrationally when spending their money. The *Financial Times*'s Lex column noted in 2008:

> It pays to be sinful in a downturn. Analysis by Merrill Lynch shows that, during the six recessions since 1970, alcohol, tobacco and casino stocks have, on average, returned 11% against a 1.5% loss for the S&P 500. Incredibly, these sectors not only had superior earnings growth but also, in five out of the last six recessions, cigarettes, booze and gambling stocks actually increased absolute earnings.

People do not forgo other types of luxuries either. Häagen-Dazs, an American ice cream-maker, saw sales soar in the recession of the 1990s. People still take holidays, though perhaps they just take them closer to home. Butlins, a British holiday-camp operator, reported a bookings increase of 15% in summer 2009. In the last quarter of 2008, British consumers spent 8.1% more on confectionery and sugary snacks. Match.com, an international online dating site, reported a 35% increase in new sign-ups in 2009. In the UK, cinema and theatre attendance and DVD rentals also increased in 2009. In the United States, cinema attendance fell by 5% in 2010, but that was while the economy as a whole was recovering. Second-hand bookshops reported a sharp increase in business. Sales at charity shops were 5% higher in 2008 than in 2007.

Harvard Business School academics John Quelch and Katherine Jocz have dug deeper into the ways in which different groups of consumers react to changing circumstances. They report their observations in two articles, "How to Market in a Downturn" in *Harvard Business Review* (April 2009) and "Managing in a Downturn" in a *Financial Times* supplement ("Keeping a Keen Eye on Consumer Behaviour", February 2009), though they use slightly different terminology in each for describing new segments of consumer generated by the recession:

- Naysayers – "frightened consumers who have stopped buying any discretionary purchases and are trimming their daily purchases".

■ Short termers – "younger, urban consumers with few savings who have, therefore, lost little in the financial meltdown". They change little in their purchasing behaviour until fired; then they change overnight.

■ Long termers – "consumers who see the reduction in their retirement accounts as an unfortunate bump in the road". They amend their behaviour slightly rather than shutting off altogether, and are sensitive to better value. They are "worried but not panicked".

■ Simplifiers – these include "baby boomers who have lost a significant percentage of their savings". They have more to worry about. They are changing their attitude to risk. Quelch and Jocz distinguish between those who are deciding to postpone retirement, and those who are just deciding to make do with less – though this suggests that further segmentation in the model is needed.

■ Sympathisers – "savvy consumers who switched into cash ahead of the crash". Generally, they are continuing to spend as before, but perhaps have decided not to buy a new car even though they can afford it because "they do not want to appear ostentatious".

■ Permabulls – the "relentlessly optimistic" whose "appetite for consumption remains constrained only by the availability of credit".

When cash is tight it is to be expected that value-for-money segments of the economy do well. In the 1930s, GE, Kellogg and Procter & Gamble all grew out of value-for-money strategies that gave customers more for less. In 2008 and 2009, low-price retailers such as Lidl benefited. Whichever way consumers are segmented and labelled, the crucial point is that not all consumers will react to a recession in the same way. Thus for entrepreneurs with insight into how different groups of consumers behave, there will always be profitable opportunities to exploit.

What is true of consumers is also true of the business-to-business sector. The demand for some goods and services increases when times are bad. Just as pawnbrokers and loan sharks thrive when consumers are short of cash, any companies that can help cash starved businesses stay solvent by cutting costs and increasing margins should be in demand. Outsourcing will seem a more attractive proposition if it reduces costs for customers. And because more organisations go bust, in recessions there are more fire sales, opportunities to acquire plant, machinery, people and businesses at a deep discount. All customers give serious thought to change during recessions. No long-standing customer relationship should ever be taken for granted, especially when customers themselves are under pressure. Businesses that fail to recognise this are at risk from those that do – as well as from opportunistic entrepreneurs.

Other external factors

■ **Demographic and sociological changes.** The changing age profile of populations in the West has enormous implications for organisations big and small, both as suppliers of products and services to a changing population and as employers. Changing levels of education can improve significantly the supply of human resources, which in turn can facilitate growth. Western universities are full of East Asian students, but universities in China and India are rapidly catching up. At the same time, technology companies in the UK complain of a shortage of appropriately qualified British employees, even in the depths of a recession. Similar claims are made frequently by employers in the United States, particularly when seeking to justify increases in the cap on visas for non-US employees – though research suggests that employers are more influenced by the fact that non-US employees are happy to work for less, another important demographic issue. Changing levels of education can also significantly change patterns of demand. Changes in patterns of migration provide opportunities for growing businesses – as the increase in the number of businesses catering to the number of commercial migrants from Eastern Europe into the UK bears witness.

■ **Technological advances.** These impose change on the economic
environment with significant implications for growth. The
life cycle of IBM illustrates the evolution of one organisation
as a consequence of technological change. IBM grew as a
consequence of following, if not indeed initiating, the rise of
the computer and its application in business and commerce.
But other organisations, notably Microsoft, were far quicker in
following the trend towards desktop computing, and then from
hardware to software, as the principal source of value in the
IT industry. While seemingly core components of IBM, such as
its PC business, have been sold, the company has developed
successful advisory and consulting services. Technological
changes in one industry frequently have implications for others,
as parallel technological changes have a habit of stoking each
other and converging. Technological change impacts growth
in other ways too. The millennium bug, whether founded on
fantasy or fact, generated an enormous amount of economic
activity around the world in the years leading up to 2000; the
development of the internet and ecommerce has provided
growth opportunities for new and old businesses – as well as
sounding the death knell for others.

■ **Political changes.** These can be as important as cyclical
economic changes. More widespread prosperity in Brazil is
largely a product of relative political stability in recent years.
Growth in China is certainly a direct consequence of changes in
attitude in the political elite and the relative economic stability
that has resulted. Such changes in the West are less radical, but
they should not be discounted. Politicians can foster a positive
climate for entrepreneurship far more directly than economists,
or even bankers.

4　Growth barriers

ANYTHING THAT IMPEDES the facilitators and drivers of growth highlighted in the previous chapter is a potential barrier to growth, and just because the business is growing does not mean that such barriers are not present and limiting the growth rate. When times are good, barriers to growth and other organisational weaknesses are often hidden; but when times are harder they may become all too apparent and have a devastating effect. In formulating their plans, managers should identify potential as well as self-evident barriers to growth, distinguishing between those that are internal and those that are external.

Internal barriers

"More businesses die from indigestion than starvation," David Packard writes in *The HP Way*, suggesting that internal issues rather than an inability to generate new business are the most awkward barriers to growth. Lack of new business is rarely the biggest barrier to growth faced by successful entrepreneurs. This is not to diminish the importance of sales to a growing business. To qualify for the label "entrepreneur", business founders are usually good salespeople in the first place. Entrepreneurs have to be confident in their ability to keep their businesses well fed. But because they tend to be obsessed with the top line, they pay insufficient attention to the increasingly sophisticated engine rooms that they need to support growth. A growing top line may make a business appear successful and healthy to outsiders, while management and staff are only too aware that on the inside the organisation is suffering from all sorts of growth pains. It is useful to bear in mind the maxim turnover is vanity, profit is sanity and cash flow is the only reality in any business, especially for a rapidly growing business.

There are several types of internal barrier to growth that a business may have to overcome when seeking a cure for organisational dysfunctionality or "indigestion". As well as those discussed implicitly in the previous chapter, the most important are:

- personal barriers related to the founders and their roles;
- people management barriers associated with the function and management of senior and middle management teams, and the remuneration of individual members;
- structural barriers associated with reporting lines and communication channels;
- cultural barriers associated with change.

When leaders get in the way

If it is accepted that businesses need to change as they grow, it should also be accepted that the roles of those who set businesses up need to change too. Indeed, as they will have been around the longest, and will have steered the initial activities and set the style of the business, nothing is likely to need to change more than the roles of the founders.

In a *Harvard Business Review* article in December 2002 John Hamm, a partner at VSP Capital in San Francisco, argues that the qualities that make for successful entrepreneurs often end up being weaknesses in chief executives in established businesses. The single-mindedness and focus that are so important in the early days can turn into the tunnel vision of a chief executive determined to take no notice of the fresh thinking brought by new members of the management team. Loyalty to those who were instrumental in establishing the business can become a liability when the business has outgrown their capabilities. The pragmatism and task-orientation that distinguishes entrepreneurs from inventors and dreamers can easily metamorphose into an obsessive attention to detail and a reluctance to delegate when they try to run their business with the help of a professional management team. The informal, can-do, personal style that was instrumental in establishing the flexible culture in a young business may not adapt to the necessarily greater bureaucracy of the larger business.

Business founders also need to acknowledge why they founded the business in the first place, and the extent to which their personal motivation is becoming a business constraint. Those who wanted to escape from a big business to run their own show will find themselves, if successful, running the same sort of venture they wanted to leave.

If business founders do not want to or cannot change, they should acknowledge that it is a question of when rather than whether they should pass the baton to someone else. J.K. Galbraith distinguishes between "corporations in which age, size and simplicity of operation still accord power to an individual who has control of capital and those where the technostructure has taken over". It is rare for entrepreneurs to find themselves sitting on top of the latter. Indeed, as Galbraith puts it in his book *The New Industrial State*:

> *The great entrepreneur must, in fact, be compared with the male Apis mellifera [honey bee]. He accomplishes his act of conception at the price of his own extinction.*

Harvard Business School professor Noam Wasserman reported in an article published in *Harvard Business Review* in 2008, "The Founder's Dilemma", that from his researches into 212 American start-ups in the late 1990s and early 2000s, by the time ventures were three years old 50% of founders were no longer the CEO. By year four only 40% remained. Fewer than 25% of founders led their businesses to IPOs (initial public offerings). Wasserman's comments serve as a warning:

> *There is ... another factor motivating entrepreneurs along with the desire to become wealthy: the drive to create and lead an organisation. The surprising thing is that trying to maximise one imperils achievement of the other. Entrepreneurs face a choice, at every step, between making money and managing their ventures. Those who don't figure out which is more important to them often end up neither wealthy nor powerful.*

When a business begins to have an existence separate from its founder – when it becomes "the" business rather than "my" business – it has reached a crucial stage in its evolution. A business that is too dependent on its founder usually finds its growth potential capped, regardless of whether the founder is aware of the need to change; the capacity and capability of even the most talented founder are not limitless. It will also be difficult to sell – when such founders walk away from their businesses a significant amount of their value goes with them. Separating founders from businesses, although a necessary component of many growth strategies, is difficult and risky. The founders of sandwich retail chain Pret a Manger, Julian Metcalfe and Sinclair Beecham, recruited an executive with first-class credentials, Andrew Rolfe, to implement their international expansion plan. Metcalfe's first action was to take a three-month holiday, not just to get some well-earned rest but also to give Rolfe space to establish his authority.

A more interesting situation is when founders step back into their businesses if the delegation of authority to incoming management proves unsuccessful. Rolfe left Pret a Manger in 2003 after a couple of years of successful growth, followed by fundamental disagreements about future strategy in the light of subsequent poor business performance. Metcalfe stepped back in as "creative director", a role not found in any governance handbooks. But Metcalfe did not intend to run the business; he appointed another individual, Clive Schlee, to manage the turnaround. Steve Jobs of Apple is another founder who stepped out (in his case after a row with the board in 1984) only to step back into the role of CEO in 1997, a year after NeXT, the company he had founded in the interim, was bought by Apple, by which time Apple's own position had deteriorated. Unlike Metcalfe, who appointed someone else to the role of CEO, Jobs took the top seat himself, and subsequently led a spectacular turnaround in Apple's fortunes. Interestingly, however, when Jobs took six months' leave for health reasons in 2009, observers worried about the future of the business, even though Apple was by then one of the biggest listed companies in the world. It is as if Jobs's relationship with Apple had changed little as the business had grown. Commentators noted his obsession with design, and his enthusiasm for the micro-management of parts of the business in ways more often associated with CEOs of much smaller businesses.

People – and the management of them

Growth barriers caused by founders can be addressed by refreshing and adding to the capacity and capability of the management team. This is easier said than done.

"If you want a job done properly around here you have to do it yourself" is a sentiment widely expressed by senior management in many businesses. The inference is that good staff are difficult to find; the reality is that the sentiment betrays a reluctance to delegate. Ask to see the organisation chart in many young owner-managed businesses and you will eventually receive, fresh from the drawing board, a diagram showing all members of the team reporting directly to the founder. The first task for those serious about growth is to unplug the top end of many of those reporting lines and plug them in to a team of professional managers who can take the business to the next stage of its evolution and thus free the founder to focus on other matters.

Senior managers, rather than working on the assumption that no one else can do the job properly, should accept that doing the job themselves is at best a temporary fix for a short-term problem. They will give themselves the best chance of managing growth if they accept that one of their roles is to make themselves redundant and to recruit people who can do the senior management job better than they can. Unfortunately, even those who think the right thoughts about delegation make the mistake of thinking "what this business needs is someone else like me". This is the essence of the brief given to many headhunters and recruitment consultants by successful senior managers (business founders in particular) anxious to build the senior team fast. Teams that are most likely to be future-proof are built out of differences in personality, constructive disagreement and creative abrasion – individuals that complement each other rather than seek the easy life through complimenting the founder. This means recruiting a team fit for building tomorrow's business rather than running yesterday's business, a team with different sorts of people, not just more of the same.

New people brought in to help manage a business will not relate to it in the same way as the founder, and will need to be motivated and managed in different ways. If this is not done, the team that has been constructed to eliminate one barrier to growth will itself become another barrier. As John Katzenbach and Douglas Smith state in their book *The Wisdom of Teams*,[16] the performance of a group of people thrown together will not even add up to the sum of its parts without significant team management effort on the part of the business founder; whereas a well-managed and effective team will give the business the capacity not only to put out the fires that need fighting from time to time but also to pay attention to the bigger picture. Team management is addressed more fully in Chapter 7.

Recruiting complementary team members has implications for the existing team members, who will have to give up some elements of their roles to outsiders. Some find this hard. New team members find it hard as well. New managers will have been brought in for their ability to take the business to the next stage of its evolution, but what they find in the meantime may come as a shock – a step back in their careers. They may have been oversold the role in the first place by founders and managers proud of what they have done so far and keen to boast about it.

As well as having different expectations from existing managers, new managers often feel differently about remuneration. They are more likely to expect a decent salary. First-generation managers may be satisfied by the excitement of founding a business reinforced by options or equity; managers with the experience of building and managing a big business expect to be paid properly, probably more than existing managers. This is a common cause of tension between different generations of management in a growing business.

Remuneration is not the only source of tension. For example, once a firm has grown to a size that warrants the recruitment of its first HR manager, it is often not long before the HR manager has become HR director, and supervises a compensation and benefits manager and a recruitment manager, each with assistants and their own budgets. In parallel, other managers in the business, as they build their own management infrastructures, begin to offload people-management problems to the HR team.

Businesses find that matters that used to be part of the portfolio of general management skills are compartmentalised; good people management is now the responsibility of HR; sales management is the preserve of the sales department; and so forth. The infrastructure that has been built to support the needs of the business has given line staff and managers the excuse to retreat from good people management, and from personal interaction with clients and customers. The structure itself has become a barrier, not just to growth but to good business. This in turn will lead to another reconstruction of senior management, this time one that attempts to reconnect managers with their people and clients. Specialist HR, sales, marketing and operations departments are not closed down – the organisation is now too big to do without them – but their roles are repositioned along the lines of internal consultants so as to support line management rather than substitute for it.

People management barriers exist in big companies just as much as in small ones. Indeed, they are so important in companies with ambitions to grow that they merit a chapter of their own (Chapter 7). But it is important to note that growth means change, and change means changing people – their roles and their behaviour. The reason change in a business can be so difficult is that for it to happen every individual in the business must change too. Everyone is different, approaching change with different preconceptions and experiencing it differently. Individuals who choose not to change will be replaced – including, of course, senior management.

Organisational structure: two dimensions

Organisational structures are both solutions to and barriers to organisational evolution and growth. A new business does not need a structure. However, a business will not be able to take advantage of the benefits of scale without structuring itself appropriately. Different structures suit different businesses at different stages of their development, and struggling on for too long with last year's structure will constrain growth.

There are two dimensions of structure to be considered: corporate and management. Corporate structure refers to the relation between the various reporting units in the business: divisions, subsidiaries and other group entities. Management structure refers to reporting lines between individuals, in particular the composition and functioning of board and board committee members, board committees, other senior managers and directors.

Different countries have different approaches to management structure, which are in turn reflected in and influenced by governance regimes that differ from country to country. In the United States and the UK, the focus of authority is a unitary board, comprising executive and independent non-executive directors. In the United States, normally an all-powerful chief executive has executive authority and is also responsible for chairing the board. In the UK, in big companies at least, the roles of chairman and chief executive (or managing director) are separate, with the former responsible for managing the board and the latter for running the business. In the UK, the separation of the role of chairman and CEO is a principle of corporate governance that listed companies must comply with or explain why they have not. There are no such restrictions in the United States.

Management structure and corporate structure are interrelated. Big businesses in Germany are obliged to have separate supervisory and management boards. Even though in the UK the unitary board structure is favoured, many companies recreate a supervisory/management board structure by having a management company (directed by one board) owned by a holding company (directed by another board), thus using a corporate vehicle to structure management.

Family businesses often adopt a similar approach as they grow. One of the rites of passage they go through is the recruitment of professional non-family managers and the delegation of responsibility to them. This rarely occurs without tension between family and professional management over involvement in if not control of the business. Some of the largest family businesses have resolved this with a dual-board structure, with the family having seats on the holding company board but leaving the subsidiary management company board to the managers. Which decisions need to be referred from one board to the next is carefully identified and codified in constitutional documentation, giving the board of the management company the flexibility to do their jobs while keeping the family sufficiently involved.

Spider plants, spaghetti or hierarchies?

As a company grows it has to pick and choose between structures. Every structure comes with advantages and disadvantages.

Turning a simple founder-led business into a complex hierarchy seems to require little more than the addition of layers of management, thus extending the reach of the organisation and management's ability to control its ever-expanding resources. The founders may or may not continue to sit at the top depending on whether or not they stand down (see above), but the organisation grows from a single starting point. It is often tightly constructed, with clear chains of command and a strong locus of power in the senior management team. However, an organisation constructed on these lines does not have to grow much before it becomes very different from the one the founders created. The ends of the chains of command are a long way from the centre. Though disciplined, such organisations can be slow moving and find it difficult to respond to changes in the market or the economy. Customer-facing parts of the organisation find their authority restricted, but this may not matter in a stable business in which customers have simple expectations. In many industries customers are no longer so easily satisfied. More typical is the business that grows from a small one in which customers value dealing with the boss, to a big one in which they feel that customer care has been compromised.

The problems inherent in a multilayer hierarchy usually encourage growing businesses sooner or later to decentralise management processes, and to build management and corporate structures that facilitate this. A business might be subdivided by product type or geography, for example, or just broken down into smaller, decentralised units. Each unit is typically granted authority to take decisions on matters that might previously have been the responsibility of the senior management team. Such organisations are flatter than traditional hierarchies. They are also more flexible and more responsive to customer needs, as the decision-takers are closer to customers. This type of structure will generate internal competition, which should help sharpen quality; but competition might degenerate into destructive backstabbing, with bits of the organisation acting in their own interests rather than those of the organisation as a whole – a problem that is particularly likely when ambitious managers are more interested in extending their personal fiefdoms than implementing corporate strategy.

The corporate structure may follow the management structure, with each division set up as a company with its own board, and maybe its own back office. However, it is easy to see under this arrangement how management costs can spiral; indeed, a new CEO seeking to turn around such a business might want to strip out pockets of "redundant" management and pull some back-office functions into a central service centre. An opposite reaction might be to sell off divisions, exchanging stand-alone businesses for cash to reinvest in those that remain. A business that grows by building and delegating to divisions is not unlike a spider plant, and one consequence of its flexibility is its ability to deconstruct itself piece by piece. Again this distinguishes it from a more tightly constructed hierarchical business.

There are compromise structures that might sit between traditional hierarchies and decentralised, divisional structures. A matrix structure attempts to retain both the discipline of the hierarchy and the flexibility and decentralisation of the divisional structure (see Figure 4.1).

In such a structure a senior finance manager, for example, in a division reports in two directions: to the CEO of the division and to a group head of finance in head office. Divisional CEOs in their turn report to a group CEO. Such organisations can quickly become complicated, and managers may find themselves caught in the middle. On the positive side, the structure itself will force the debates that matter to the surface: debates between the centre and the division, and between those responsible for setting corporate strategy in pursuit of growth and those responsible for clients on a daily basis. Such structures also help to expose managers with a tendency for building personal fiefdoms at the expense of corporate objectives.

Some organisations, taking advantage of the connectivity offered by computer systems, have invented even more radical structures: networks of individuals connected to each other virtually; and organisations in which people report to each other variously depending on the project – for example, A might report to B in one project while

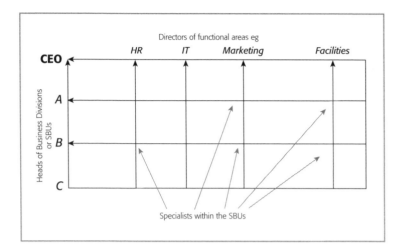

FIG 4.1 A matrix structure

simultaneously B might be member of another team led by A. For an increasing number of organisations structure is fluid, continuously adapting to meet current circumstances. Boundaries between different types of staff and different types of activity are losing definition, as are boundaries between work and play, employment and self-employment. Even boundaries between client and service provider are becoming blurred as project teams include client representatives and suppliers; customers up and down the supply chain adopt open-book costing and accounting strategies; and industries adopt lean manufacturing and just-in-time supply chain processes. Organisations are reaching towards stranger metaphors to capture what they are trying to achieve with structure, such as "upside down management" and "the spaghetti organisation".

Nypro, a plastics mouldings business, has worked hard to create flexible management and corporate structures that have sustained rather than obstructed growth. With headquarters in the United States, 18,000 employees around the world in 49 locations in 16 countries, and a turnover of more than $1 billion in 2008, Nypro is a big business. But it is also privately owned by its employees. Nypro is unusual in the way in which it approaches the structuring of local management. Regional businesses are run by a board of directors comprising senior staff drawn from other businesses in the organisation. This fosters a sense of co-operation between businesses across the organisation. Remuneration strategies also encourage co-operation. Performance-related remuneration is determined by the performance of the team, not the individual. Project teams include client representatives, thus ensuring client interests are recognised.

At the same time, Nypro has a strongly competitive streak. Teams and businesses compete with each other. The organisation's strong flair for innovation is driven in part by the competitive culture. An obsession with client service also plays a role, as does the fact that good ideas developed in one part of the business quickly find their way across the business, not because of command and control, but because of the determination to be best and the fact that senior managers find themselves responsible for several teams, if not several companies, within the organisation. Indeed, Nypro's culture is a curious balance between co-operation and competition that is supported by the way it structures itself and its management.

In family businesses the need to deal with family issues adds another layer to an organisational structure that is probably complicated enough already. Well-managed family businesses work hard at identifying and analysing family issues and business issues, determining where they reinforce and undermine each other. Such businesses are often as "businesslike" about family issues as they are about business issues, forming family councils and constitutions to manage such things as remuneration for family members, recruitment and, most important of all, succession planning from one generation to another.

In many ways most family business problems are sophisticated manifestations of a problem that faces all growing businesses: understanding and managing the difference between control and ownership. Sorting out the structure is often an important part of the solution.

Reluctance to change

As the coverage of organisational issues in this chapter and of growth models in Chapter 2 make clear, a reluctance or, worse still, an inability to change is a substantial barrier to growth.

A growing business needs to anticipate the future and prepare for the challenges of the next stage of evolution. This may require changing something that is not yet broken. The faster the business is growing, the more likely it will need to change, but the more difficult it will be to make the case. Much of the reluctance to change, therefore, will be the fault of management responsible for yesterday's success. In his book *The Prince*, published in 1532 (five years after his death), Machiavelli is as pertinent as ever about change:

> It ought to be remembered that there is nothing more difficult to take in hand, more perilous to conduct, or more uncertain in its success, than to take the lead in the introduction of a new order of things. Because the innovator has for enemies all those who have done well under the old conditions, and lukewarm defenders in those who may do well under the new.

Much has been written on change management, but for growing businesses the following principles are important:

- When time is tight or you have a crisis on your hands, a top-down, strongly directed approach is often best. But do not expect the experience to be happy.

- When time pressure is easier or when a business is doing well, a bottom-up, participatory process is better.

- For a business with ambitions to grow it is as well to keep change permanently on the agenda. Like tai chi, it may not be comfortable but will keep you supple as you get older.

Given that a growing business is a business that is doing well, change is most likely to be successful if it is a bottom-up, participatory process, in which those involved or affected have a sense of ownership of the change initiative, than might be the case if change is imposed. Similarly, a business ambitious for growth should find ways of keeping change on the agenda, ensuring last year's successes do not turn into next year's sacred cows. In their article "Change for change's sake" in *Harvard Business Review*, Freek Vermeulen and Phanish Puranam of London Business School and Ranjay Gulati of Harvard Business School argue that seemingly healthy well-performing companies can be vulnerable because of a build-up of what they call "corporate cholesterol". Such organisations should make sure that they use more than one type of change to clear it, otherwise the process of change may become routine. Growing organisations that do not look for change as a matter of course eventually find themselves cornered in a crisis, and the only way out is a top-down, directed, painful and expensive change programme.

External barriers

It is easy to blame a failure to grow on external barriers. Many external barriers are propped up by internal ones, the most common involving people. For example, for every company that complains that a lack of finance is preventing growth, there is an organisation in the business of providing finance emphasising that it invests money in management teams not businesses – and so a company wanting to raise money should ensure its team is robust. In many instances the barrier is not the lack of finance but the capability and attitude of the people behind the business – for example, a reluctance to take on debt or equity on the part of owner-managers. Conversely, external barriers may be seen as opportunities that will – or could – provide a springboard for further growth.

Nevertheless, there are external barriers to growth beyond management's sphere of influence. In some industries there are institutional and regulatory barriers that prevent organisations growing; and organisations attempting to sell to some markets find that external factors limit their size. Such factors include the following.

The personal touch

Markets that demand the "home-made" or "personal" touch present particular challenges to growing businesses. Those that succeed in selling into these markets often find themselves dependent on one or two pivotal members of the company. How businesses work at converting personal characteristics such as personality and individual skill into corporate characteristics such as brand and organisational culture is discussed in Chapter 7. Some businesses have worked particularly hard at adjusting automated mass-production processes to replicate the characteristics of hand-made processes. Batch-made premium potato chips are described by some manufacturers as "hand-made" in the UK, while in other parts of the world manufacturers describe them as "kettle-made". In both instances processes will have been developed to continuously rake the chips to prevent them from sticking together. But there will come a point when the fundamental mechanics of production or of just doing business will run out of process innovations. Either growth will falter or essential qualities of the product or service will change. Businesses that revise their product or service in these circumstances risk a lot in the name of growth, particularly when they see other, smaller businesses move into the hand-made, personal-service space they have vacated.

Other businesses look for scale in replication, ensuring that the essential unit of the business itself stays the same size and seeking growth through increasing the number of units. Pret a Manger makes sure that sandwiches are always made on site. Each shop has its own kitchen, adding significantly to the fixed costs of the business as a whole but enabling it to maintain claims about the freshness of its product and also to cater better for local demand.

Prestigious constraints

Premium brands face other market-related barriers to growth. Exclusivity, although it allows a business to charge more, may in turn become a barrier to growth. Only 444 Ferrari 550 Barchettas were initially planned, though 448 eventually appeared, largely because of Japanese superstitions about particular numbers. Producing the vehicle in significantly larger quantities would have risked damaging the perceptions of the famous marque – and might not have been any more profitable because of the lower prices that would have been charged for the cars. Indeed, Ferrari on occasions works hard at making the already exclusive even more exclusive. In 2009 it announced that it would produce just five Ferrari 550 GTZs based on the Barchetta in conjunction with Zapato. All five cars were sold for £1m ($1.6m) each before the official announcement. For Ferrari less is more; its most important growth measure is the perceived increase in the brand's prestige. Ferrari will never be a big company by any of the measures of size and growth discussed in this book.

Many prestige propositions inevitably, therefore, address small markets. The size of a prestige market itself is a barrier to significant growth. Product diversification may open up new market segments and therefore appear to provide routes to growth, but in following them management run the risk of damaging the prestige brand itself. Conversely, big players in an industry might try to acquire small, niche, prestige businesses, believing they can add resources and investment and bask in the reflected glory. Again, both businesses run the risk of doing each other damage, and the strategy seems to fail more often than it succeeds. Ford has had a long and chequered history buying exclusive car manufacturers and then living to regret it, including most recently Aston Martin and Jaguar. In the 1960s Ford thought it had done a deal to acquire Ferrari, only for the owners of the Italian company to pull out at the last minute. (A consequence of this was the production of the Ford GT40 sports car, designed to beat Ferrari at its own game. The GT40 went on to win at Le Mans for four consecutive years.) In the car industry, Volkswagen now owns Bentley and also appears to have won plaudits for its work with the Bugatti brand, though in truth it did little more than buy a defunct name with a glorious history.

The growth problems associated with premium brands do not always stop with small niche companies. Mercedes-Benz has always been much bigger than Ferrari, but it has successfully built a premium brand proposition on a reputation for quality and reliability. Daimler-Benz's 1998 merger with Chrysler was a deal all about growth, but as a strategy it failed. The costs of investment and the management effort required to bring Chrysler up to European standards drew resources and management attention away from the core German business, jeopardising the brand qualities that made Daimler-Benz successful in the first place. Even before customers started questioning the quality of their new Mercedes, market observers were talking about the damage the Chrysler tie-up might do to the Mercedes brand just by association. The CEO of Daimler-Benz admitted the deal had been a failure at the St Gallen Symposium in 2008, a year after selling Chrysler for $1:

The reality was that we couldn't actually achieve global integration because it was at odds with the image of our brands, the preferences of our customers, and many other success factors – all of which were far more diverse and fragmented. It's fair to say that we overestimated the potential of passing leading-edge technology from Mercedes-Benz to Chrysler. Unlike premium brand customers, American volume brand customers are far too price-sensitive to absorb its cost ... In the final analysis, we learned a practical lesson about the limits of globalisation.

The company also learned an important lesson about growth.

Growth planning – aided by SWOT and LEPEST

Companies should identify their growth drivers and barriers and make sure that their implications are accounted for in their business plans, specifying where a business is now and how it plans to grow in the future. The simplest way of evaluating growth drivers and barriers is through a SWOT analysis (strengths, weaknesses, opportunities and threats). Strengths and opportunities are both categories of growth driver. A strength is an internal capability in the business and an opportunity is a characteristic of the external commercial environment; management can take advantage of both when planning for growth. Unlike a strength, an opportunity for one business is an opportunity for other businesses as well. Weaknesses and threats, however, are categories of growth barrier. Mirroring strengths and opportunities, a weakness is an internal characteristic of the business and a threat is a characteristic of the external commercial environment.

Opportunities and threats, both characteristics of the external environment, can be identified through brainstorming, benchmarking the competition and monitoring customer feedback (see Chapter 3). The mnemonic LEPEST (or PESTLE) is often used to remind managers to consider legal, economic, political, environmental, sociological and technological influences on the commercial environment of the business.

Strengths and weaknesses, both characteristics of the internal organisation, are much more under the control of management and reflect their choices as much as their capabilities. As Albus

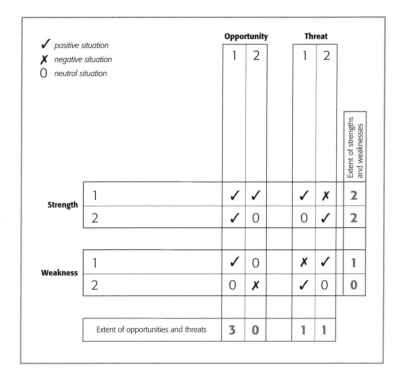

FIG 4.2 Internal strengths and weaknesses matrix

Dumbledore says to Harry Potter, "It is our choices that show what we truly are far more than our abilities." Bearing in mind the issues discussed in this chapter, a list of strengths and weaknesses can be assembled through an honest internal assessment of organisational capabilities, reinforced by competitor analysis and benchmarking. Analysis using the growth models in Chapter 2 will help tease out hidden weaknesses, particularly weaknesses exacerbated by the changes generated by growth and the recent evolution of the business.

Many business managers are familiar with SWOT analysis. Surprisingly few, however, go on to the next stage and ask "So what?" about their SWOTs.

One way of exploring the implications of lists of internal and external strengths and weaknesses and opportunities and threats is to match them against each other using a simple matrix (see Figure 4.2). Each strength is matched against each opportunity. If a strength helps you take advantage of the opportunity, it is marked with a tick; if it has nothing to do with the opportunity, it is marked with a zero. A strength might go some way towards ameliorating a threat, in which case it is marked with a tick. In rare circumstances, a quality that managers consider to be a strength might become a weakness when a particular opportunity is considered; in this case the appropriate box is marked with a cross. Similarly, if a strength does nothing to ameliorate a weakness, it is marked with a zero; but if it makes things worse, it is marked with a cross.

A similar exercise can be undertaken for weaknesses. The existence of a weakness might prevent an organisation from taking advantage of a particular opportunity, in which case it is marked with a cross. A cross is also used to indicate when a weakness exacerbates a threat. If a weakness is irrelevant as far as any particular opportunity or threat is concerned, it is marked with a zero. As with strengths, there might be rare circumstances in which a quality normally perceived as a weakness turns into a strength when considered in the context of a particular strength or weakness. Generally, however, strengths should be scored with lots of ticks and a few zeros, and weaknesses with crosses and zeros.

Adding across the row will give managers an indication of the importance of a strength or weakness, given the opportunities or threats confronting an organisation. This may help them decide where to prioritise resources. Many management teams take comfort in, boast about and waste investment in nurturing a strength that has little relevance to the circumstances in which the business finds itself. Businesses in markets that are subject to disruptive innovations are particularly susceptible to this tendency, failing to invest in the competencies that the changing market now values. Adding down the column will give an indication of the importance of an opportunity or a threat given the current portfolio of strengths and weaknesses at the organisation's disposal.

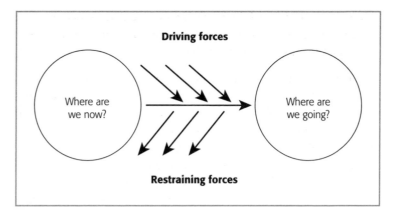

FIG 4.3 Force-field analysis

Accentuate the positive; eliminate the negative

Taking SWOT analysis to this second stage is not the only way in which management teams can identify the implications of their growth drivers and barriers. As an alternative, or indeed a complement, to working on specific opportunities and threats, they may focus on an overall strategic goal using a version of a technique used in the social sciences called force-field analysis (see Figure 4.3).

There are three things management teams need to do:

■ Have a clear vision of what the organisation is trying to achieve. There should be a robust analysis of where the organisation is now and the extent to which organisational reality falls short of the target.

■ Identify what is holding back the organisation from the achievement of its targets, and what positive qualities it possesses. In the model such forces are often labelled driving forces and restraining forces, but they might just as easily be called growth drivers and barriers. This work can be delegated to middle or junior level staff, who often have a clearer picture of organisational reality than senior management.

■ Identify actions that will accentuate and foster the growth drivers, and reduce if not eliminate the barriers. Again, such an exercise can usefully be delegated. If staff are allowed a role in the identification of actions, they are more likely to be committed to implementing them.

Identifying real, grassroots actions is the best way of effecting change in any organisation. Talk of targets and workshops that lead to the identification of strengths and weaknesses, driving and restraining forces, growth drivers and barriers are all very well, and will give managers plenty of excuses for arguments, but it is actions that can be implemented in the real world that will ultimately make the difference. If an organisation succeeds in implementing just a proportion of the actions it has identified, it will succeed in moving towards its targets and realising its growth ambitions.

The growth plan itself: principal contents

Before the D-Day landings Eisenhower observed, "In preparing for battle I have always found that plans are useless, but planning is indispensable." It is certainly the case that the only thing that can be guaranteed about any business plan is that reality will not turn out that way. Even so, planning is still a useful exercise as it will help identify and focus attention on growth levers and barriers.

Business plans can be drafted for many reasons, seeking to raise finance being an important one. Many big businesses have a regular long-term planning cycle, which is the starting-point for annual planning and budget processes. Regardless of their purpose, most business plans have elements in common (see Table 4.1 for a checklist of business plan contents).

A business plan for growth – a growth plan – might also include many if not all the items listed in Table 4.1, as well as addressing the growth levers and barriers identified in Chapters 2 and 3. Managers planning for growth should also pay particular attention to the following:

■ The ambitions of owners and senior managers. Plans for growth should consider the key individuals involved in the business. Such individuals' aspirations will change and they may not share the same ambitions, so a growth plan should consider their ambitions and capabilities, and how differences between them can be reconciled with the plans for the business.

■ Focus. Planning for growth is often not so much about identifying growth levers and barriers as picking which ones to focus on.

■ The management bottleneck. Plans for growth should pay particular attention to alleviating the barrier to growth created by the capacity and capability of management.

■ Organisational change. Growth is about change, and planning processes for growth need to anticipate the changes that growth will bring. Careful use of one or other of the growth models discussed in Chapter 2 can help.

■ Changes in the competitive environment. Much business analysis focuses on current rather than future competition. The competitive environment for a growing business changes all the time. Success will bring new competition, which should be anticipated and a response planned.

■ A framework for monitoring and measuring growth (see Chapter 5).

■ Cash costs of growth. Growth consumes cash at a rate that can take management by surprise. Planning is all about anticipating surprises, and there are few more important than this one. It merits a separate chapter later on.

Table 4.1 Business plan contents

1 Executive summary

■ Summary of customer needs and how to address them	■ Financial consequences of plan
	■ Finance required

2 The business and the opportunity

■ Customer needs addressed	■ Make or buy considerations
■ Product descriptions and applications	■ Sources of supply and security
■ How business operations convert custom into cash	■ Plant needed
	■ Proprietary position/barriers to entry
■ Manufacturing process	■ Guarantees and warranties

- Reliance on third parties
- New product development plans

- Corporate structure
- SWOT analysis

3 Industry, market and competitors

- PESTLE analysis
- Market and segment size and growth
- Industry structure: five-forces analysis
- Current and potential competitors
- Customer decision criteria
- Target market segments (showing differentiation from competition)

- Marketing strategy
- Pricing policy
- Choice of location and premises
- Distribution channels
- Competitor response
- Market share projection
- Sales forecast

4 Selling

- Current selling method
- Proposed selling methods

- Sales channels
- Sales resources

5 Management and staffing

- The management team
- Other principal human resources
- Specific management roles for existing and planned staff and general organisation of the business

- Planned recruitment and selection
- Reward packages and their relationship to the required business performance
- Training and development plan

6 Mergers & acquisitions, joint ventures, divestments

- Logic for acquisition
- Target profile

- Plans for search

7 Actions

- Principal actions, showing responsibilities, costs, deadlines, dependencies, priorities

- Milestones
- First-year actions outlined in more detail

8 Financial data and forecasts

- Summary of financial performance ratios: return on investment, etc
- Summary forecasts: profit and loss, cash flow

- Assumptions underpinning financial forecasts
- Key performance indicators
- Sensitivity analysis
- Risk mitigation

9 Financing requirements

- Current shareholders, loans outstanding
- Funds required and timing, including leasing
- Use of proceeds

- The deal on offer
- Anticipated gearing and interest cover
- Exit routes for investors
- Appendices

Appendices

- Biographies
- Names and details of advisers
- Technical data and drawings
- Patents, copyrights, etc
- Audited accounts
- Consultants' reports
- Published data on product, market, etc
- Orders in hand and enquiry status
- Detailed market research methods and findings
- Organisation charts
- Sources of data

5   Measuring and describing growth

MANAGERS SET ON a path to growth must first decide what they are seeking to grow and how they will measure their achievement. When plotted on the same graph the various measures that can be used will not necessarily move in parallel, which suggests that there are different types of growth that respond to different levers.

Growth is the difference between measurements of size taken at different times. Big companies with less room for further growth are less interested in growth, but they are interested in measurements of size and in their position in the pecking order relative to other big companies. This chapter discusses some of the methods used to measure size and growth.

Revenue, turnover and sales

International Financial Reporting Standards refer to revenue in their treatment of sales revenue. In the United States, the terms revenue or gross sales are used, whereas in the UK turnover is the term commonly used. Revenue appears at the top of a company's income statement (profit and loss account) and has the nickname "the top line". Thus a business whose revenue is growing is exhibiting top-line growth. The number on the top line is easy to spot, and a business ambitious for growth will help substantiate growth claims if it can show consistent growth in revenue. J.K. Galbraith called revenue growth the "*sine qua non* of growth". The term "turnover" suggests the rate of activity in a business, the speed with which the engine of a business is turning over. The revenue figure in the accounts, however, is a product of price and volume. It is possible to show an increase in revenue by increasing prices while volume stays the same, or even decreases. Furthermore, increases in revenue mean more in relative than in absolute terms. An increase in revenue also needs to be considered in the context of the rate of inflation.

Revenue, along with other measures discussed in this chapter, is sensitive to changes in accounting policy, and accounting, particularly management accounting, is more an art than a science. Accountants and regulators and the interpreters of accounts worry about "revenue recognition" in particular. For example, when is a sale booked as a sale: when the order is placed? Or when the payment deposit is received? Or when the product is delivered? Or when the outstanding money has been paid? When devising performance measures for the use of internal management these questions need to be answered.

The published financial statements of American companies are subject to more prescriptive rule-based accounting approaches, which provide answers to questions like these. But there are regular complaints that the application of US GAAP (generally accepted accounting principles) can lead to accounting presentation that is contrary to common sense, let alone commercial sense. It is not unusual for a sales team to close a deal that they consider to be in the commercial interests of the business only to find it cannot yet be included in the published financial statements. When preparing the internal management accounts that are used to run the business, companies all over the world are left alone to come up with practices that enable management to best do its job; and the practice selected for management accounts might well differ from that demanded by the regulators for published financial statements anyway. In the UK, even when preparing published financial statements, different companies will answer these questions in different ways and reach different answers when adding up their sales.

When companies trip over accounting policies the consequences can be serious. In July 1998 Allied Carpets announced accounting irregularities. Its published policy was to book a sale on delivery. But some stores had been encouraged to book sales on payment, slightly earlier in the business cycle. Compared with other companies in the industry, whose policy was to book sales on the receipt of a deposit, Allied Carpets' new and unofficial practice, as well as its published policy, were considered conservative by outsiders. But the company's failure to adhere to its own policy led to the suspension of its shares, the spending of hundreds of thousands of pounds on financial investigations and the resignation of at least two senior managers. Interestingly, such a change of policy (at least before its discovery) had no direct effect on the timing or amount of cash collected, or on the volume of goods sold.

Assuming the same accounting policy is applied consistently from one year to the next and business is fairly consistent, different policies are unlikely to have much impact on published numbers in the long term. But a change from a conservative revenue-recognition policy to a less conservative one might have the impact of increasing reported revenue in one year.

Revenue is a measure of how much product or service is being shifted and for what price, but it says little about the efficiency of the operation, its ability to turn sales into profit and then cash. A business that grows revenue but pays insufficient attention to profit and cash measures is one whose growth is likely to be unsustainable and whose future is uncertain. Revenue is vanity, profit is sanity, cash flow is reality.

Market share

If the market is growing it must be easier, in theory if not always in practice, to grow the business, so the growth of a business should be considered in the context of its market and industry. Big businesses that dominate their industries consider market share an important measure as it indicates the success of the business compared with the competition. For businesses in such a position an increase in relative market share is as good a growth measure as any. Different parts of a company's business (analysed by geography, category or product) have different characteristics and generate different profit levels, so getting the mix right is important.

Profit/income: gross and net

No business can survive in the long term without profit or income (as it is referred to in the United States). When assessing an opportunity, entrepreneurs rightly worry about market and industry size, and the ability of the founding team to build a healthy revenue top line. Top-line revenue growth figures, percentage of invitations to tender converted to real business, and so on, all matter. Revenue is easy to understand, but an understanding of profit – the "bottom line" – and how it relates to revenue, demands an appreciation of the other factors contributing to the income statement, including pricing and costs. Sales people understand sales, but successful business managers understand margin. In a manufacturing business, raw materials need to be purchased, salaries and overheads need to be paid, factories need to run and the whole operation needs to be financed before profit can be made.

On the assumption that all businesses exist to make a profit – or at least have an ability to generate profit – most would argue that profit is an important measure of success. Many would argue that profit is a more important measure than revenue, and that growth in profit is more important than growth in revenue. Growth in profit may well come as a consequence of business decisions that lead to decreases in revenue. Businesses wishing to cut costs often seek to cut staff, which might then mean the withdrawal from less profitable or unprofitable lines of business. The organisation might end up much smaller than it was, but if its profits have increased, in one important sense the business has grown.

There are different types of profit. Gross profit (turnover minus cost of sales – that is, the costs directly attributable to each sale) and gross margin (gross profit as a percentage of sales) indicate the health of the essential engine that underpins the business. Businesses in different industries have different gross profit profiles, so gross profit should best be used to measure the performance of a company's product or service against projections and against similar businesses in similar industries. Different products sold by the same company will have different profit profiles. Wise managers know that they should be wary of favouring high-margin products within their business portfolios just because they are high margin. High-margin and low-margin products and services often have symbiotic relationships within the same company. Gillette makes more profit on the refills for its shavers and its shaving accessories than on the shaver itself, but it would be foolish for the company to focus only on refills and accessories. Similarly, printers are cheap because the manufacturers make their money on ink cartridges. Service businesses, which have few raw materials costs, are inherently more profitable than manufacturing businesses. A business that assembles and installs automatic doors will also want to sell the contracts for maintaining the doors. There are instances of companies fighting to secure a position in a market by underpricing and selling products or services at a loss.

Gross profit is profit after deducting the costs directly associated with the sale. It ignores the costs associated with back-office functions: the overheads. Gross profit is a measure of interest to companies in the same industry that may wish to buy the business; they may see much of the back office doubling up resources that they already possess. Deciding which costs to deduct when calculating gross profit is often a matter of judgment. Net profit (and net margin – net profit as a percentage of revenue) is profit after all costs, including back-office costs, have been deducted. Net profit indicates the ability of a business to generate a return. Calculating net profit before deducting tax, interest or depreciation (earnings before interest, tax, depreciation and amortisation or EBITDA) is common as this focuses attention on the cash-generating capability of the business. Tax is an allocation of profit rather than a cost that is incurred to generate it. Similarly, interest is an appropriation by a stakeholder (a creditor) rather than a cost incurred in keeping the wheels spinning. Depreciation is an accounting entry rather than a cash cost.

Managers who focus on profit as well as turnover or market share are acutely aware of the importance of price, perhaps more so than volume. There is often the temptation to underprice rather than overprice in the desire to win business. Getting the price right at the outset therefore is critical; it is a lot more difficult to increase it afterwards. One approach to increasing sales is to cut prices. But a price cut goes straight to the bottom line, and the operating model of the company will multiply its effect. For example, a business making a 10% margin decides on a 5% price cut to boost sales. It had been making $10 on every $100 of sales; now it makes only $5 on every $95 of sales. A 5% reduction in price has led to a 50% reduction in margin. Revenue will have to more than double to make the 5% price reduction worthwhile. Conversely, raising prices – or at least ensuring they keep pace with inflation – is the easiest, cheapest and quickest way of increasing margin.

Rigorous cost control as a route to increasing profit can be less risky than increasing prices – at least a business does not have to speculate about the impact of its decision on its customers – unless cost cuts mean a poorer product or service. Some industries have been revolutionised by new entrants that have focused on fundamentally rethinking the cost side of the business. Southwest Airlines was one of the first of many low-cost airlines. It ran only one type of aircraft to minimise the costs associated with maintenance, training and turnaround. It focused on short flights, thus reducing the costs associated with meals. It chose to fly from small airports rather than big international ones with high landing charges, and focused on the segment of the market that was more interested in getting there than in getting there in style.

But cost management can spring surprises. In many businesses, particularly knowledge businesses, the most significant costs are the costs of staff. Keeping down staff salaries might be at the expense of increasing staff turnover, which in turn will increase recruitment and training costs. Similarly, striking a hard bargain with suppliers might make enemies in the industry that a business could well do without, particularly when new competitors enter, or when it is looking for favours. As is often the case, short-term cost control measures can have unanticipated long-term consequences.

Determining profit is even more subjective than determining revenue, being influenced by accounting regulation and policy and the choices made by management. Whether or not to capitalise expenditure – that is, enter it on the balance sheet as an asset rather than write it off against revenue as a cost on the income statement – can have a significant impact on reported profit. In some instances, there is not much of a decision to make. If a company buys a freehold property, it will capitalise it; the investment will then sit on the balance sheet and the consequent depreciation charge will hit the company's profit. In many instances, however, the decision to capitalise can be a matter of judgment. Title Research, when setting up its genealogy search business, findmypast.com, spent approximately £1m ($1.6m) digitalising births, marriage and desk records. After discussions with their advisers, the managers decided to write off the investment costs, as there were significant uncertainties associated with the new business. This reduced the profit (and tax) for the year. When selling the business several years later, the managers needed to persuade buyers that the book value of assets on the balance sheet significantly undervalued the business because it did not include the digitalised data sets from which the business was still earning money.

Just as an undue focus on revenue can lead to an unsustainable growth path, so can an undue focus on profit to the detriment of other measures damage a business's long-term prospects. Profit in the short term can be increased by cutting costs. Taken too far, cutting costs will compromise the long-term growth of the business. Indeed, some might argue that to an extent growth and profit are contradictory objectives. In the short term, in many businesses it is possible to increase profit by slowing down the rate of growth. There is a balance that needs to be found, and finding the point of balance involves an assessment of a complicated knot of variables both inside and outside the business. Ultimately, finding the point of balance is, once again, an art rather than a science.

When considering profit as a measure in the growing business it is important to examine the concept of break-even. When a company, or a business within the company, breaks even it has reached a size sufficient to cover its fixed costs and make a cash contribution. A business's break-even position may be expressed as a formula: fixed costs divided by gross margin. For example, a business venture has fixed costs of $100,000 a year and a gross margin of 25%. Its break-even position is therefore $100,000 \div 0.25 = 400,000$. In other words, when sales reach $400,000 a year the business will break even. The concept of break-even is important in a growing business. Break-even is a crucial moment in the evolution of a business and the relationship between financial stakeholders and management. It also highlights the importance of margin or profit. The healthier the margin, the quicker break-even point will be reached and the easier it will be to sustain profitability.

Different parts of a company's business (analysed by geography, category or product) will have different characteristics and will generate different profit levels, so getting the mix right and understanding its implications is important when assessing profit.

Headcount

Headcount, the number of staff on the payroll, is one of many measures that gauge the extent of the resources deployed by the organisation. Some businesses might be more interested in measures that reflect other assets in the business, for example capital employed or resources consumed. Government bodies use headcount as an indicator of an organisation's size. A bigger business generally employs more people; more people to manage presents management challenges that businesses with fewer people to manage can avoid. Headcount is therefore for many industries a good proxy for the size – and complexity – of an organisation.

It is a good, but by no means perfect, measure. When times are good, businesses often recruit ahead of the growth curve; when times are bad, they often cut back on human resources in anticipation of lost business. Revenue and headcount curves do not move in parallel. Besides, different types of industry have different human resources requirements. A property business can trade in property portfolios worth billions of dollars with only a handful of staff; other industries are far more people-intensive.

As with revenue, an organisation's wage bill is influenced by price (that is, salary levels) as well as by headcount. Headcount is the more sensible measure of growth, but total employment cost is an important measure as well. An early indication of the changing fortunes (changing for the worse, that is) of a business ambitious for growth is a declining value added per employee $ ratio (gross profit ÷ employee costs).

The most important constraint on growth is management capacity and capability. Some of the most frequently used business performance measures assess returns on critical resources. Rather than measure return on equity or return on invested capital, why not measure return on management? Robert Simons, a professor at Harvard Business School, has argued in favour of attempting this as it would focus management's attention on where it can add most value, but the measure would need to be qualitative not quantitative.

Employee turnover, or the rate at which employees are leaving the business, is also a useful measure in a growing business attempting to increase its headcount. It is not sufficient to be good at recruiting new staff; a growing business also has to be good at retaining staff.

Growth: the shareholders' perspective

Revenue, profit and headcount measures consider the performance of a business from the inside out. But for those who believe that a business exists to generate returns for the owners or shareholders, the most important measures are those that look at the company from the owners' perspective. Growth for shareholders means an increase in the value of their shares. This reflects the dividends and other cash payments paid to shareholders, which are underpinned by business fundamentals, which might take an analyst back to profits, revenue and headcount.

Assessing shareholder value and shareholder return is a discipline in itself. When assessing the returns that a business generates from the point of view of the shareholder, it is important to consider alternatives. Just as in a big business revenue growth should be considered against the growth in the overall market, so returns to a shareholder should be considered against what those funds might have earned if they had been invested in risk-free securities. At the very least shareholders should be entitled to expect better returns than that. Business valuation methodologies often attempt to take account of the risk inherent in the business and put a value on the anticipated cash flows likely to accrue to shareholders accordingly.

The share price of a listed business is an obvious indication of its worth, reflecting the value the market puts on future dividends. But even in a listed business, value is a more slippery concept than the share price might suggest. A listed company wishing to take control or buy another listed company will often have to pay a premium to persuade enough of the shareholders to give up their shares. If more than one acquirer is interested, the price might go higher still.

Private companies

In private companies valuation is even more complicated. As there is no market for the shares they are less liquid, which makes them less valuable. There is no real-time external market mechanism for assessing shareholder value. There are consultants who, for a decent fee, will be prepared to value the company, and such exercises are common, particularly when employee equity and share-option schemes are involved.

Before attempting to value a business, it is important to determine who wants to know and why. If a company is not expected to continue trading but is to be broken up, any value it might have will be tied up in what can be realised from the resale of its individual assets. Some of these may have been used as security for debt and thus will be of little value to the shareholder. When a company is being valued as a going concern, its value is tied up in the future ability of the business to generate cash. Valuers might express this in terms of a price/earnings or P/E ratio. Some might consider the prices paid recently for businesses in the same industry and how these prices compare with the profits made by the business, and use the formula so derived to calculate a value for other companies. Others might attempt to assess the future cash flows of the business directly, and then discount these using a discount factor reflecting the perceived riskiness of the business (the riskier the business, the higher the discount factor and the lower the resulting value – or the higher the cash flows needed to satisfy the investor). But any such calculation is fraught with subjectivity: the valuation is highly sensitive to changes in the discount factor, which itself is determined on the basis of some well-educated guesses about the future of the business and the industry; and then there is the reliability of the business plan from which future cash flows will have been derived.

Ultimately, shareholder value in a private business can be determined with certainty only when a price has been agreed for selling the business. The value of anything becomes meaningful only when it is converted into a price that is acceptable to a vendor and an acquirer. At that point two sets of shareholders, the old and the new, have reached an understanding as to what the business is worth (usually leaving both parties feeling slightly hard-done-by).

People businesses and partnerships

When owner-managers sell a business they withdraw their own contribution to the business, and this may have a significant downward influence on the business's value. This is seen clearly in professional services firms, which are often structured as partnerships rather than companies. The partnership model suits industries, usually people rather than asset intensive, in which the association between the owners and the business is important. In professional services firms, despite the knowledge-management revolution, most of the business's assets are often in the heads of the partners.

A partnership allows individuals to take advantage of scale, and the efficiencies to be derived from working in close proximity with people with complementary skills, but it is still in essence a collection of individuals each with personal relationships with a set of clients. It is significant that many partnerships take their corporate name from the names of the founding partners. The implications of this are often misunderstood, even by partners, and particularly by those in knowledge businesses who have converted their partnerships into incorporated entities, and who thus own share certificates that give their owners the illusion that they own a share of a business that has a value separable from themselves. (Just as there are large partnerships that are in effect run as corporate entities, so there are limited companies that are really still partnerships both at heart and as a matter of commercial reality.)

This comes to a head when partners, particularly founding partners, with their names on the door, seek to retire. For many, the prospect of retiring involves a presumption of "selling" their share of the business to the junior partners. Far from being grateful for the opportunity, many junior partners in these circumstances argue that the retiring senior partners are trying to have their cake and eat it. If their personal role has been so considerable, it and its value will leave with them on their retirement. They cannot have it both ways: if they stay, they are of value and will earn well; if they go, they will enjoy their retirement but will not earn, and will not be rewarded for any "value" left behind in the business because there will not be much. In essence, therefore, many people businesses, regardless of their legal form, are not mechanisms for aggregating value, they are mechanisms for distributing income. The most significant financial capital that is needed in many people businesses is working capital: capital is not needed to finance assets, and surplus financial capital does not find it so easy to earn a return, which again has implications for stakeholders who define their objectives in terms derived from more typical shareholder-company models.

The "consolidator" phenomenon in the accountancy industry illustrates how the partnership model and the relationship between partners, the business and financial stakeholders work. Accountancy is a profitable industry, and financiers have circled it for years wondering how to get a piece of the action; or rather, imagining that there is some action that it would be interesting to get a piece of without having to worry about the perils of owner-management. After all, a partnership that makes money, and that is so inherently scalable (just add more people who are good enough to find new clients), is surely a decent investment proposition.

In the past few years, financiers have been spinning the wheels on just such a model. The thinking has had a defensible logic: create a business vehicle; list it on the stockmarket; and use the money raised to buy up smaller practices around the country. Smaller practices are constrained by lack of resources. Membership of a bigger, better-financed entity would give them reach and resources that would otherwise be unobtainable. Furthermore, partnership capital is illiquid: you cannot realise it until you retire, and then you have to find someone willing to finance the withdrawal of your capital. This is likely to be existing partners or individuals promoted to the partnership to fill your chair, but neither might leap at the opportunity. If you are close to retirement, faced with limited alternatives, you might be tempted by the opportunity to exchange your partnership for cash and marketable shares in a listed entity.

But for many, the reality has been very different from the dream. Numerica, with Levy Gee as its largest member firm and "base tenant", raised $40m in the markets and set about acquiring and consolidating smaller accounting practices around the country. But the wheel turned. After a difficult period of trading, Numerica itself was swallowed up by a bigger spider, Vantis, another of the consolidators.

In Australia things have turned out even worse: consolidator Harts Australasia and Stockford collapsed in 2001; and another, Garrisons Accounting Group, was placed in administration in 2003.

Why the difficulties, particularly given the undoubted profitability of the industry as a whole? Some partners, now directors or other types of employee in a listed entity, take the view with hindsight that they were sold a pup. The share options that many of them took (rather than free equity or cash) tied them in rather than offered them realisable value. Even those holding real paper were obliged to watch it decline in value as the consolidators failed to make an impression on new investors. The model was troubled for other reasons. Decision-takers in partnerships are often partners who are close to retirement; but the partners on whom future business depends are often younger partners, whose earning potential continues to be tied up with the future of the business. Some consolidator deals were made by older partners who took the money and looked forward to imminent retirement, but the partners who were left to do the work were left also with the prospect of having to share their returns with financial stakeholders.

Some have defined the problem as old partners retiring unfairly at the expense of junior partners. But it goes further than that, as firms seek to recruit junior staff at the bottom of a machine that ultimately depends for its success on its ability to develop senior staff and partners in the future. Why join a practice where the future earnings potential is reduced? As noted above, partnerships of knowledge-management professionals are mechanisms for sharing income, not for appreciating value. Another reason the decision-takers in firms selling to consolidators might have wished to sell was that their income had not been sufficient to support their expectations. For them, the consolidator model was a ticket out; for the consolidator, the model had the effect of attracting firms that had not been successful enough to realise their ambitions on their own. They have ended up with senior staff frustrated at sharing business returns with financial stakeholders.

The real issue is that value in a professional services business is achieved very differently from that in most shareholder-owned businesses. This can be seen in the way that many professional services firms choose not to account for goodwill when measuring equity value. In other words, a partner's equity stake in a business is valued only as the capital introduced into the business by the partner and the partner's share of the profits, which have yet to be taken out. No value is attributed to the partner's share of the business itself. When such a business is acquired, any value placed on the business in excess of this is also attributable to the partners, but the fact that many businesses refuse to account for such value themselves should serve as a warning to any potential acquirer of the dangers of overpaying. What is true for professional partnerships is true to varying extents for many other knowledge-based owner-managed businesses.

External shareholders

From the perspective of external shareholders who are not owner-managers, it is important to distinguish the value of an investment to the shareholder from the value of the company. The two are not necessarily the same. Share values for listed companies go up and down with the market as well as being influenced by turnover, market share and profitability. Many shareholders, though technically owners of a slice of the business, behave as if they are owners of their portion of capital, which they have given to the company for a return. Shareholders in this sense are inclined to behave like debt holders rather than equity holders.

In recent years, and particularly since the economic collapse of 2008, there have been calls for recognising the interests of a broader range of stakeholders rather than giving too much priority to the interests of shareholders. There is a lot of sense in this. Too much attention paid to shareholder interests to the detriment of other stakeholders has not been in companies' long-term interests. When the interests of management become too closely aligned with those of shareholders, usually by way of equity incentives for managers, companies have paradoxically found short-term gain taking priority over long-term sustainability. If you want management to act in the interests of shareholders, some have argued, take away management's shares.

Alternatively, management might be set the task of satisfying the goals of the broader group of stakeholders. This sounds good in theory, but is difficult to achieve in practice and even more difficult to measure. One reason the CEO of a listed company finds it easy to focus on shareholder value rather than stakeholder value is that increases in shareholder value are much easier to measure. Theorists cannot even agree about which of the rest of the stakeholder group they should be worried about, let alone how to measure growth in returns to them.

Range and depth

Many new ventures start with one service product, and often just one client or customer. An important task for a new business team seeking to build a sustainable business proposition is extending the range of the business's products and services and its number of customers and clients. The range and depth of an organisation's business are thus important elements of a successful growth proposition.

As is often the case, the proposition can work in reverse. Many a management team talks about the 80:20 rule: that 80% of its revenues or profits come from 20% of its customers or products. Successful growth comes, therefore, not just from acquiring new business, but from acquiring the right kind of business.

Other measures

There are other measures of growth, many reflecting unusual characteristics of the industry in which the company operates. Oil companies may be interested in the volume of barrels of oil produced, or filling stations opened; a record company or publisher in copies sold, or royalties earned, or prizes won, or titles published. Many organisations work towards certifications of quality: ISO9001 in the UK or the Baldrige Award in the United States. Some organisations have taken unusual approaches to assessing their success.

Skandia, a multinational financial services company based in Sweden, generated a lot of publicity when it attempted to measure elements of its intellectual capital including its "competence base" (defined as employees' professional insights, applied experience and organisational learning) and "performance procedures" (defined as how its customers are handled, and how its operations, processes, business development and logistics are conducted). In the UK the prime minister, David Cameron, has expressed a wish to measure national happiness. The Kingdom of Bhutan already claims to measure gross national happiness. Many large companies attempt to measure employee satisfaction and corporate well-being, principally using quantifiable outputs from employee attitude surveys.

In general, any organisation keen to demonstrate how well it has done will choose to highlight some measure by which it can be judged to have done so.

Difficulties of assessment and interpretation

In young businesses, measuring all aspects of performance, including growth, has its own challenges. When preparing management information, it is immediately apparent how much standard accounting relies on the historical record and on policy and practice. New businesses do not have any history. It is difficult to interpret trends in a young business in which good business practice has not been established and therefore cannot be relied on. Young growing businesses change more quickly and more fundamentally than established ones; the assumptions behind an accounting policy are likely to date and therefore the policy will need to change. Whether or not to write off expenditure or to capitalise it is a matter of judgment and policy. There are detailed rules governing how a business should answer this sort of question when drafting public financial statements, particularly in the United States. But new businesses have to determine their management accounting practices as the business model evolves.

In owner-managed businesses, regardless of size, the line between the owner-manager and the business becomes blurred, making it difficult to isolate and assess the performance of the underlying business. Whether a private business makes an accounting profit or just breaks even is often a matter for the owner-manager and the tax authorities. Owner-managers might charge to the business expenses that might be disallowed in a big business, not because they are illegal, but because when the business is yours you do what suits you best provided it is legitimate. In young businesses, financial performance as recorded in the accounts is often distorted in the other direction. Business founders often do not take a salary or a return from the business in the early days. Either way, the true costs of doing business are often not reflected in the financial records.

It is naive to assume, particularly when businesses are growing, that it is possible to confine the measurement of growth to a single measure. Companies that focus too intently on one measure run the risk of dysfunctional performance. American academic Chris Zook notes that companies that grow revenue but not profit do not create value in the long term; however, companies that grow profit but not turnover are on an unsustainable growth path. Companies that grow revenue and profit but do not earn their cost of capital run out of investors. Zook's list is not meant to be complete. Growing companies should worry about management capacity and infrastructure, as well as maintaining an asset base sufficient to support sustainable growth. Managers in pursuit of sustained growth should keep their eyes on a range of dials on their dashboards.

An added complication is that some business activities are easier to measure and assess than others, and there is no corollary between ease of measurement and importance. As Einstein noted, "Not everything that can be counted counts, and not everything that counts can be counted." Items that have human activity at their heart can be particularly difficult to assess. Big numbers like revenue and profit help present a broad-brush picture, but it is the detail that matters.

The complications of change

Another factor is change. In a business that is evolving as well as expanding, new product or service lines can have a significant impact on both performance and the nature of the figures reported. A manufacturing business that introduces customer service and product maintenance will find that the dynamics of the business model changes, so the basis of a new set of numbers showing increasing profit needs careful analysis. Change has implications for accounting policies, which might need to be adjusted to reflect changes in the underlying business model.

It can be difficult therefore to measure growth either side of a change of strategy or accounting policy or the introduction of a new line of business. For example, the performance of some large companies in the years preceding the credit crunch were buoyed by the profits earned by their financial services divisions. On April Fool's Day 2008, Porsche was reported as having published figures showing that sales had plummeted 27%; but the company reported increased overall profits, notwithstanding the decline in car sales, thanks to the performance of its financial services division.

Furthermore, although managers often project steady and smooth growth, in practice it rarely happens linearly, the reality being a series of steps and lurches. A business investing in the next stage of its development may put pressure on its margins until the investment starts to pay back. Fixed costs and variable costs are never as clearly distinguishable from each other as accountants would like. Fixed costs (overheads) can be cut or increased. Again, adding to overheads usually happens in large steps. Conversely, variable costs are rarely as variable as their label might suggest. Components and resources are often sourced in bulk to achieve economies of scale. Accountants might smooth the reported purchases figure in the accounts by taking account of the movement in stock or inventory, but the underlying reality of the business is anything but smooth.

Then there are the consequences of mergers and acquisitions. Organic growth on its own is difficult enough to measure, but combining two organisations introduces further distortions. Lines of seemingly similar accounting information in two different organisations rarely reflect identical activities. Combining two organisations carries its own integration costs. Expansion overseas brings complications caused by fluctuations in exchange rates, different tax regimes, different ways of doing business – including attitudes to payment and employment – and different attitudes to accounting practice. The net effect is that it can be difficult to measure growth from one period to the next.

Pace and capacity

Another important variable is the pace of growth. Businesses can grow at the wrong speed. Businesses that grow too slowly might lose advantage in the market to competitors. Those that grow too fast might lose control with dangerous consequences across several dimensions. Toyota's rapid expansion up to 2009 has been blamed for the safety issues that led to the recall of at least 8.5m vehicles. Ahead of an appearance before a US congressional hearing, the company's president, Akio Toyoda, conceded that the firm's growth "may have been too quick". Toyoda suggested that the company's "priorities became confused" as the carmaker grew. Toyota's reputation suffered as a consequence of a sequence of major faults across different types of product, including faulty accelerator pedals and braking systems. A business growing too fast is also one that risks losing the confidence of its staff. Driving an out-of-control business is just as scary as driving an out-of-control train, with every chance of it ending in disaster. Businesses that grow fast put pressure on their cash resources (see Chapter 6) as growth consumes cash, which must be found from internal operations or from external financiers. Businesses go bust, not because they do not make enough profit, but because they run out of cash.

What is an acceptable level of growth? There are three simple tests:

■ Growth is financially acceptable if management know in advance how it is going to be financed (see Chapter 6).

■ Growth is strategically acceptable if it continues to secure and enhance the company's position in the industry and marketplace.

■ Growth is operationally acceptable if management know how it will be controlled and supported.

The first test is about financial capacity. The second test is about management's real understanding of the business. Sock Shop was one of the UK retailing sensations of the 1980s, selling socks and hosiery from small outlets in locations with a high footfall such as underground railway stations. Following initially modest growth plans, the business grew rapidly, but when it expanded from the London Underground to the New York subway, and then onto the high street, Sock Shop found itself in difficulty. Trading underground in New York proved far riskier than trading underground in London. On the high street, where rents were higher and competitors included established high-street retailers, Sock Shop found it had to reinvent its business model. Its customers changed too, with more considered, price-conscious purchasers replacing the business people rushing to buy socks or replace laddered tights before a meeting in the City. By 1990 Sock Shop had called in the administrators. Thus an essentially sound business that was misunderstood by its owners was sold – only to go bust again in 1996, and again in 2006.

The third test is about management capacity. Robert Simons proposes an interesting framework for assessing the business risk faced by a growing company, which also captures the complexity inherent in the business.[17] The business risk calculator – tested, Simons claims, by "managers from hundreds of different companies" – invites managers to categorise and assess the extent to which their business is exposed to each category (see Figure 5.1).

Questions companies should ask are as follows:

- **Growth.** To what extent are managers and staff under pressure to deliver? How fast is the company growing? To what extent do managers and staff have experience of the situation in which the business finds itself? High scores indicate a company that might be growing and changing more quickly than the capability and capacity of management to control it.

- **Culture.** This section assesses some of the softer elements in a governance framework likely to be tested in a growing business. How significant to staff are their potential rewards for risk taking? How resistant are executives to receiving bad news? ("Do not give me problems, bring me solutions.") How competitive is the internal environment? High scores in this row suggest that individuals, in the interest of meeting targets, are likely to take more risks than is good for the company. They are also less likely to draw problems to the attention of management in time for them to be addressed.

- **Information management.** This section covers the complexity that comes with growth. How fast does the business engine that underpins the business turn over, and how many components are in the engine? The more there are the less likely it is that management will be aware of all aspects of the business. To what extent do the indicators chosen to measure performance capture the total activity of the business, or are there

Growth	Pressure for performance		Rate of expansion		Inexperience of employees	
	?	+	?	+	?	=
Culture	Rewards for entrepreneurial risk taking		Executive resistance to bad news		Level of internal competition	
	?	+	?	+	?	=
Information management	Transaction complexity and velocity		Gaps in diagnostic performance measures		Degree of decentralised decision making	
	?	+	?	+	?	=

Source: Simons, R., "How risky is your company?", *Harvard Business Review*, May 1999

FIG 5.1 The business risk exposure calculator

fundamental gaps? How decentralised is decision-taking? Have controls been put in place to supervise the managers to whom authority has been delegated, or have senior management in effect confused delegation with abdication?

The three rows in Figure 5.1 and each item within them are interlocking. High scores in all sections suggest a business that is growing fast, is becoming more complicated and is not under the control of management. Simons proposed his model in 1999, but his lessons have not been taken to heart. No one at Enron or Andersen paid much attention. Nor were there many low scores among firms that came unstuck during the global financial crisis, such as Lehman Brothers and RBS.

6   Financing growth

THE CAPABILITY AND capacity of the management team are the most important drivers (or enablers) or barriers to growth, but without the necessary financial resources growth will be impossible to achieve. A crucial capability of a management team is its ability to raise – and conserve – finance.

Generating and managing cash

The most discussed sources of finance for a business are external, in the form of debt or equity, but the first place to look for cash is inside the business itself. Every business should be a machine that generates cash. Most businesses can be forgiven the occasional lapse, but over the longer term a business's operating model must be strong enough to convert sales opportunities into cash. As well as generating cash, a business must look after it effectively. This requires skilful management of the balance sheet, making sure that cash flows through the business as efficiently as possible and that the balance sheet is not unnecessarily weighed down with assets such as trade debtors and stock or inventory, which might otherwise be converted to cash.

Business managers who are good at managing cash are aware of how much cash is tied up in various parts of the business and how long it sticks there; and they are good at clearing unnecessary blockages. If the nature of a business means it has to keep stock or inventory, this will lengthen the time it takes to convert raw materials or purchases into cash. In some businesses, such as bookshops, stock is slow moving. In others, such as supermarkets, it moves much faster. Some businesses, notably service businesses, do not need to tie up cash in stock at all. If customers and clients of businesses in an industry routinely pay for products up front (as they do for the products of most retail businesses), cash will come into the business fast. But businesses that depend for their income on customers who can dictate lengthy payment terms may have to wait for cash to come in.

Businesses that pay their suppliers immediately are at a cash flow disadvantage to those that pay their creditors on terms. The longer a business can keep cash in the business, the less it has to rely on external sources for the cash to finance the business. The timing of cash flows in and out of a business is never entirely at the discretion of management, but management teams that do not pay attention often find themselves paying their bills too soon. Big businesses can and do often dictate payment terms to small businesses. When the recession struck, some big businesses told their customers that they expected payment within two weeks rather than 30 days. Most businesses, even big businesses, find it easier to bully their suppliers than their customers. In autumn 2008 Tesco, the UK's largest retailer, wrote to its non-food suppliers to inform them that it wanted to change its payment terms from 30 to 60 days with effect from December 1st. In a statement, Tesco said:

> This is a move to align payment terms for our larger non-food suppliers across the Tesco group which currently vary from country to country and within product categories. We have written to suppliers to seek their agreement to the change and hope to implement it before the end of the year.

Most suppliers, anxious to keep the Tesco account, would not have regarded the letter as an attempt to "seek their agreement". The consequence of the change of terms was to improve Tesco's working capital and cash position at the expense of its suppliers. Tesco is not alone. Frank Garson II, president of The Loveable Company, a supplier to Walmart, said of the latter in an interview given to Fast Company:

> They have such awesome purchasing power that they write their own ticket. If they don't like your prices they'll go vertical and do it themselves – or they will find someone who will meet their terms.

The Loveable Company had had a contract with Walmart that Walmart had unilaterally revised, forcing Loveable to give up the business. Three years later, Loveable went under. "Walmart chewed us up and spat us out," Garson said.

It is often assumed that cash management is something that small businesses are more likely to get wrong. Maybe, but the basics of cash management are as true for big businesses as for small businesses, and they can go wrong for big businesses too. When Travelex completed its acquisition of Thomas Cook Global Financial Services for £400m ($640m) in March 2001, it established that it could run its new acquisition with £130m ($208m) less working capital than the previous management. In effect, £130m-worth of cash was sitting unnecessarily on the company's balance sheet. This made a significant contribution to Travelex's repayment of the loan to buy the business in the first place.

Cash management is intrinsically related to the effective management of margin, which in turn is closely associated with cost control. Early-stage businesses that have plenty of cash are rare, so tight control of costs is crucial. Most start-ups have to make do with less cash, or with none at all. Start-ups are usually advised never to buy up front what can be paid for in instalments or on credit; never to pay on credit for what can be leased or hired at sensible rates; never to lease or hire what can be borrowed for nothing; and not to be afraid of looking a gift horse in the mouth if it appears, swallowing pride and saying "thank you".

Effective cost management requires a ruthless examination of the detail and an ability to distinguish the critical from the merely useful. Companies that are growing successfully need to protect their margins. Big companies might enter the market at a discount. Suppliers of product or raw materials might put up their prices in order to share in your success. Success might mean a move to more expensive premises in a better location. Big companies that want to strengthen their cash position, however, will work hard at reducing costs as well as adjusting the timing of their cash flows. Whether or not to pay a dividend and how much the dividend should be is a bigger issue for listed businesses than it is for private ones, especially those that are owner-managed, because of its relation to share price, but it is also about cash conservation.

As has been suggested, sometimes cost and cash management pull in different directions. Offering discounts to encourage swift payment on the part of customers may speed up the flow of cash into the business significantly. But such discounting can cut heavily into margins and goes straight to the bottom line. Too often, customers, particularly big ones, take the discount and still pay late, so their suppliers lose both ways. The converse is also true of purchase discounts. Taking advantage of a purchase discount by paying suppliers quickly might well improve margins (though not as much as choosing not to offer a sales discount), but it might put pressure on a business's cash resources as cash will have to leave the business sooner.

Managing the investment in growth

Growth is costly. In the long term growth may be the only way to secure a sustainable business, but in the short term it will cost money. A growing business must reinvest in itself and will need increasing amounts of working capital (the amount of resources tied up in the balance sheet in the cash cycle). A manufacturer will need to invest in raw materials, some of which will sit on the balance sheet. It may have to offer payment terms to its customers, in which case trade debtors will sit on the balance sheet as well. To a certain extent working capital pressures from stock and debtors may be lessened by payment terms taken by a company from its suppliers, but for many companies the terms they obtain from their suppliers are less generous than those their customers demand. When a company grows its working capital requirements increase, usually in advance of sales and profits turning into cash. Increases in working capital are at the expense of cash in the business.

Many growing businesses, especially business-to-business ones with reliable customers, take advantage of asset-based finance, borrowing mainly against debtors and occasionally against inventory as well. Borrowing against working capital is a particularly effective form of finance in a growing business as the capacity to borrow effectively grows with the business. But borrowing against working capital is often expensive. Moreover, every business has a debt capacity beyond which, if it is incapable of generating any more cash from its operations, it will be in danger of overtrading.

Those who have studied the arithmetical relationship between financing needs, profitability and growth, such as Neil Churchill and John Mullins in an article, "How Fast Can your Company Afford to Grow", published in *Harvard Business Review* in 2001, have noted that in theoretical terms it is possible to calculate to what extent cash constraints determined by cash flows in and out of a business will allow the business to grow. Their essential principles should be taken to heart by the managers of every growing business:

- A business that ties up cash unnecessarily on the balance sheet in the form of excess inventory or uncollected debtors is putting itself under unnecessary cash pressure.
- A business that is paying its suppliers more quickly than necessary is putting itself under unnecessary cash pressure.
- The higher a business's margins, the greater its cash-generating capability is likely to be.
- The faster a business grows, the more pressure it will put on its cash resources.

Growing too fast

A business that is growing too fast is overtrading. There is a savage irony in overtrading in that it is in many ways a consequence of success. In the simplest terms, a business that is overtrading is attempting to do too much with the cash resources at its disposal. It is buying more raw materials, products or employee time than it can afford to satisfy the customers and clients who have not yet paid for the products or services they have ordered. Such a business has too much of its wealth in non-cash assets, the organisational equivalent of too much cholesterol. A business facing overtrading has three options:

- To generate more cash, faster, from the business itself. This is unlikely to work. In a business that is overtrading every element is already being tested to the utmost.
- To slow down, which is also surprisingly difficult to achieve. It may require turning business down, and there is the risk of disappointing sources of future business and upsetting

customers and ambitious staff. One strategy may be to increase prices. This will have the effect of increasing the cash the business operations are generating as well as choking off some demand from customers who are unwilling to pay the higher price.

- To seek external financing, probably equity finance, as debt capacity is likely to have been reached.

Managers in successful, fast-growing businesses must look out for signs of overtrading. These include cash balances trending downwards, payment terms to suppliers lengthening and the overdraft facility being used more frequently. When the current ratio (current assets/current liabilities) is less than 1, questions should be asked about the business's ability to pay its short-term creditors; in other words, its ability to keep going.

External sources of finance

External sources of cash are needed to fund the business when internal sources are insufficient. This will almost always be the case when the business is young. It is a rare new business that requires no capital commitment and instantly generates cash. Government and other types of grants might be available, particularly if the opportunity is associated with a technology being developed by a local university, which may be able to offer the support of a local business incubator, providing relatively cheap and flexible accommodation, as well as access to professional expertise and the brainpower in the university itself.

Internal sources of finance will also be stretched when a business, regardless of size, embarks on major strategic change or a significant acquisition. As noted, such a business will need to look for external cash when its activities fail to generate sufficient cash. This might be in times of economic trouble, or when the business is overtrading.

Debt finance

Debt finance – borrowing the money – allows a company to raise cash without giving away any share capital or equity. It can offset interest payments against tax (assuming it is making enough profit to incur tax), and thus there is good reason to expect debt finance to be relatively cheap. In theory, therefore, debt finance has a lot in its favour. In practice, however, it may not be so easy to obtain – and those made cynical by bitter experience may grumble that banks are very happy to give you money when you do not particularly need it; and then when you really do need it, they are only too keen to take away what they have given you so far.

If a business is looking for debt finance, especially when times are hard, it helps to understand how banks think, and thus avoid any unnecessary misunderstanding or disappointment. Banks lend their money in return for interest. A bank will lose a lot more if the company it has lent money to goes bust than it will earn from interest if it does well. If the company does spectacularly well, the bank will be little better off. It will need to earn a lot of interest from a lot of clients to recover what it has lost on a client that has gone bust, unless it can protect itself in some way. In many ways the hue and cry against the banks in 2008 and 2009 when debt capital seemed so much more difficult to raise marked a return to sensible banking – dull, conservative, risk-conscious, but nonetheless sensible.

There are various types of debt finance.

Overdrafts
Overdraft funding is risky for the bank and for the borrower. In any business, small or large, it should be used only to fund short-term cash flow shortfalls. An overdraft can be called in at any time, so it is a high-risk strategy for a business to rely on it for longer-term financing. From the bank's point of view an overdraft is unsecured, increasing its exposure. Even though a business pays interest on an overdraft only when it has one, interest rates are high to reflect the risk. Longer-term appropriately structured debt financing will be much cheaper.

Loans against assets
When structuring debt, the most common way a bank can make sure that its position is protected is not through setting aggressive interest rates, but by securing its loan against assets in the business. If

the business goes under, at least the bank can lay claim to and sell the asset against which it has secured the debt. Asset-rich businesses find it easier to borrow money. And assets are not just bricks, mortar and machinery; intangible assets can be used as well. Raising money against trade debtors, for example, is now well established and has the added advantage of growing as the business grows (assuming the debtor book grows with the business, which is usual). However, financiers will only lend money against quality debtors. Debtor finance is unlikely to be of much use to a new company unless it is buying an established business that has debt capacity on its balance sheet, or it has a guaranteed blue-chip order book.

Borrowing money against trade debtors (receivables in the United States) is often called invoice discounting. In an alternative arrangement called factoring, a company sells its debtor book to a financier (a factor), which is likely to take over responsibility for debt collection and administration. Factoring is usually more expensive than invoice discounting.

Cash flow lending

An established business with a good track record may be able to take advantage of cash flow lending. Rather than taking security against specific assets, a bank relies on the cash flow that the business expects to generate. The bank will seek safeguards in the form of warranties and covenants based on such measures as profitability, enterprise value and ratios comparing profit with interest. If the covenants are breached, the bank has the right to recall the loan. The bank usually puts measures in place that allow it to take control of the company's cash flows if it defaults on loan repayments. Enthusiasts for cash flow lending argue that it is more focused than asset-based lending on the ability of a business to repay its debts. Focusing on an assessment of future cash flows rather than assets that can be secured often increases the debt capacity of a business. Cash flow lenders understandably are more enthusiastic about businesses that are not cyclical, although definitions of cyclicality change at various stages of the cycle. When times are good lenders are more likely to have a sympathetic view of cash flow lending than when times are bad, and banks may lend money to a company on the basis of business propositions that might otherwise be considered inappropriate for bank funding.

Corporate bonds and debentures

Big, established businesses have other debt options. A corporate bond or debenture is longer-term debt instrument with a maturity date, a redemption value and a coupon (an interest rate, usually fixed). Corporate bonds are similar to the bonds issued by governments seeking to finance (or more often refinance) their debts, but they are issued by companies rather than countries. Like the shares of listed companies, corporate bonds are often traded on markets. The market's perception of the riskiness of the debt is reflected in its market price, which in turn affects the real interest rate earned by the acquirer of the bond.

Bond markets are regulated, and raising money this way can be expensive, not least in management time. It is a moot point whether from the perspective of the issuing company this sort of financing has all the disadvantages of raising money via the public equity markets with none of the advantages, or the other way around. But a corporate bond will enable a big company to access debt without the help of a bank. This might allow it to raise money for a lower interest rate. It might also allow it to put its debt out for a longer period than a bank might be prepared to countenance. Some bonds and debentures can also be convertible into shares, with the conversion triggered either by a particular event or after a fixed period of time. Convertibility usually makes the debt cheaper. Bonds and debentures that carry higher interest rates because they are considered to have a higher risk of default are often called junk bonds.

Guarantees

Even if a business has assets it can borrow against, or can secure other forms of lending, it will still need to repay the loan and to finance the interest. Companies cannot rely on interest rates going down when expected, as many have found in recent times when official interest rates have hovered around zero. Young, entrepreneurial businesses, even if they have debt capacity (that is, assets they can borrow against), are inherently risky propositions, and the interest rate a financier will charge will reflect in part the risk inherent in the investment. The credit crunch made banks even less likely to be supportive and much more concerned with tidying up their own balance sheets than with providing finance to businesses.

Small-business owners are often asked by banks for personal guarantees that put their own (as opposed to the company's) assets at risk if the company is unable to pay back the loan, notwithstanding the limited liability status of the company. Personal guarantee documents are long and complicated, and designed to protect the bank's interests. But many of those asked to give personal guarantees pay insufficient attention to protecting their own positions before signing the documentation. A business owner should resist giving a personal guarantee and, if faced with no alternative, should take independent professional advice before agreeing to one. Wherever possible spread the burden of the guarantee by involving joint guarantors, and limit the scope of the guarantee to a maximum amount. When the guarantee (or the debt) is no longer needed have it legally withdrawn, otherwise it may be used in the future, possibly in relation to an entirely different piece of business.

Companies in the UK may be able to take advantage of government-backed debt-guarantee schemes such as the Enterprise Finance Guarantee Scheme. In the US the Small Business Administration provides guarantor services in a similar way.

Equity finance

The other principal source of finance, for businesses of all shapes and sizes, is equity, referred to as share ownership in the UK and stock ownership in the United States. A shareholder owns a slice of the business. The share entitles its owner to a share of the future income distributed by the business either in the form of dividends or when the business is sold. There are different types of shares, and the nuances are spelled out in the small print of the documentation, but the most common are as follows:

- Common stock or ordinary shares. The basic type of share which entitles its holder to all income and capital after the holders of other classes of shareholder and debt holder have been satisfied.

■ Preferred or preference shares or stock. Holders of these shares have preferential rights over the holders of ordinary shares. Typically, a preference shareholder is entitled to a dividend before an ordinary shareholder and is paid off first in the event of liquidation. Preference shareholders do not normally have a vote.

■ Preferred ordinary shares or stock. Holders of these shares are entitled to the best features of ordinary and preferred shares. Typically, they have a vote, but they also have preferential rights when it comes to dividends or liquidation. Institutions usually invest in one or other type of preferred share so that they can benefit from the increased control provided by their preferential rights.

■ Cumulative shares or stock. If dividends on these shares are earned but not distributed, the entitlement to the dividend may be aggregated cumulatively and paid out at a later date.

■ Convertible shares or stock. These are convertible into another class of share. Typically, preferred shares can be converted into ordinary shares if the investment underperforms, thus allowing the holders of preferred shares to take control of the company. Institutional investors may also invest in convertible debt – debt instruments that can be converted into shares in certain circumstances.

■ Participating shares or stock. The label refers to the right to participate in any dividend or distribution paid to the holders of ordinary shares. Otherwise, in many cases, preference shareholders are entitled to a fixed dividend only.

■ Any combination of the above. Sophisticated institutional investors cook up share instruments that have the characteristics that best suit their interests in the investment. Cumulative convertible participating preferred ordinary shares are commonly used by institutions when investing in young companies.

Different types of shareholders will want to invest in different types of shares depending on their interest in the company. Founders usually hold ordinary shares, although external investors sometimes require the founders' shares to be qualified in some way, to ensure the founders are motivated to stay in the business. In the UK, individual investors in private companies often prefer to have ordinary shares rather than any of the more complicated preferred shares as this is often the only way they can benefit from tax breaks, such as the Enterprise Investment Scheme, designed to encourage investment in small companies. Institutions are not entitled to these tax breaks and usually prefer to take advantage of the additional safeguards and controls offered by preferred shares.

Friends and family: the first to turn to

Despite the advice from seasoned entrepreneurs that the best source of finance is other people's money or OPM, the first source of equity for a start-up is usually the founder. Would-be entrepreneurs will need to give up their day jobs so that they can focus on a new business idea – though few give up highly paid jobs immediately to become first-time entrepreneurs. Andrew Palmer, founder of New Covent Garden Soup, is an exception. He gave up a well-paid job in the City to work for nothing on his new chilled soup idea. Many entrepreneurs start when they have little; they then have little to lose. Increasingly, individuals use an MBA as the opportunity to resign from one job, take stock, formulate a business plan and then start a business when graduating. Even if entrepreneurs are not investing money, they are investing a kind of capital: intellectual and commercial capital, time and money. In return for their investment they own the business, have equity in it, or are shareholders – the terms are synonymous.

Once the entrepreneur's own funds have been exhausted, new businesses often call on what cynics refer to the "three Fs" (friends, family and fools) for initial funding. One of the earliest investors in Body Shop was Ian McGlinn, a garage owner, whose initial investment of £4,000 ($6,600) in the new business ultimately turned into a 22.6% stake in a listed company worth £120m ($198m) when L'Oréal bought Body Shop in 2006. But "friends and family" often reflects the nature of the investment made in a fledgling business: emotional rather than rational, personal rather than commercial, instinctive rather than analytical. Investment in start-ups needs to be set in the context of how many of them fail. The most recent numbers released by the American Small Business Administration suggest that 30% of businesses last under two years. The failure rate for businesses based on new products, or seeking to develop new markets, is much higher.

Angels – and dragons and sharks

The first arm's length equity investments are more likely to come from an individual – a "business angel" – than an institution. Angels (often, perhaps ironically, now known as "dragons" in the UK, and "sharks" in the United States, thanks to the TV programmes *Dragons' Den* and *Shark Tank* respectively) are usually successful business people who have changed from entrepreneurs to investors. They often take advantage of tax breaks giving exemption from capital gains when investing, in the United States, in qualified small business stock. Angels in the UK can use the Enterprise Investment Scheme when investing, giving them significant income and capital gains tax benefits as long as they are qualifying individuals investing in ordinary shares in qualifying companies based in the UK. Angels often invest as members of syndicates. Their choice of investments is influenced by their personal experience; they therefore tend to invest close to home and in businesses they understand. It is important to remember that an angel will have more to offer than just money and will be able to provide valuable experience, guidance and contacts. More often than not an angel will want to sit on the board. When considering whether to accept an angel's help, senior managers need to consider whether they want the sort of support that the angel is likely to bring, or whether the angel will just get in the way. An angel might be looking for a job as well as an investment opportunity; a company might need the money but might not have a vacancy.

At the heart of much equity investment is a paradox. Institutional equity investors, including venture capital firms, often find it difficult to invest in young ventures because the founders want too little money. Angel investors are usually prepared to invest less than institutions, and at earlier stages, and in part help plug the gap. But even angels interested in spending amounts small enough to satisfy the needs of many owner-managed businesses can be difficult to find. This partly reflects the characteristics of equity finance compared with debt finance. In theory debt finance is straightforward. Can the company offer security? Can the business afford the interest and the repayments? If the answer to both of these questions is yes, debt is relatively easy to find. Equity financiers are not as comfortable with security; they look instead at the robustness of the proposition, the quality of the opportunity, the return it will generate and the business's ability to repay the investment, notwithstanding the lack of security. Such qualities are difficult to assess and the assessment process, called due diligence, takes time and costs money, which the investor must justify spending. Institutions, private equity houses and venture capitalists with sophisticated due diligence mechanisms to satisfy are therefore only interested in investing large sums. Business angels have cheaper assessment processes, but they have them nevertheless. Thus a new business often has to fall back on family, friends and contacts where business angels fear to tread.

Venture capital and private equity

Which institutions are likely to be interested in equity investment in growth companies? Venture capitalists and private equity houses at heart are the same. Both are run by management teams that seek to put together partnerships of investors interested in the high and risky returns that ambitious private companies can provide. Both will try to raise a fund; they will then invest in a portfolio of private companies for the life of the fund. By the end of the life of the fund both will have sought to have exited their investments and distributed handsome returns to their investing partners, while retaining a percentage for themselves (known as their carry) to complement the management fee they have charged throughout the life of the fund. Institutions that invest in early-stage companies are often called venture capitalists; when investments are made in established companies, or are used to fund the acquisition of a listed business (taking a company private), the investing institution usually talks about private equity.

Entrepreneurship is often associated with venture capital and private equity, but in reality private equity and venture capital provide only a small proportion of the equity finance needed by entrepreneurial businesses. This is partly because of the particular qualities that a venture capitalist looks for in an investment: rapid growth prospects, an experienced team, a good fit with the venture capitalist's existing portfolio, a clear exit route and large enough to justify the costs of investment. Most entrepreneurial investment possibilities fail on one or more of these criteria.

The last criterion is perhaps the most important. Venture capitalists are interested only in opportunities that are likely to deliver a huge return, and their hunger for such a return can lead to conflict with a business's founder. For most entrepreneurs their venture is a once-in-a-career opportunity; but venture capitalists are protected to a certain extent by the portfolio effect created by investing in a pool of investments. When times are difficult they are inclined to pull in their horns and the proportion of young businesses supported by private institutional investment shrinks further. And if they have funds available, they will be even more careful about how they allocate them.

Although it is only by investing in risky ventures that venture capitalists find the returns they are looking for, once the risky venture has been identified they work as hard as possible to "derisk" their investment, often by investing via a package of debt and equity instruments. As institutions they are less able to benefit from the tax breaks given to individuals investing in ordinary shares, so they are more likely to invest in types of preferred share, giving themselves advantages over ordinary shareholders when it comes to dividends or cash distributions resulting from sale. They also often take advantage of convertible instruments: preferred shares that can be turned into ordinary shares under certain conditions, or debt instruments that can be converted into equity, enabling the venture capitalist to seize control particularly if things turn bad. Venture capitalists often ask for board representation so that they can keep a close eye on their investments from inside the boardroom. They might demand anti-dilution provisions, protecting them in the event of a refinancing at a lower value in the future, or various degrees of involvement in certain types of management decision. They will have a keen interest in the company's constitutional documentation, including its articles of association and shareholder agreements. Their cash might be invested stage by stage depending on the achievement of certain targets. They might insist that the equity stakes of the founders are also structured on the basis of some form of ratchet, giving the founders a bigger stake when certain milestones are achieved.

The realities involved

Even if the founders still own the majority of the shares in the business they have founded, they will have given up significant influence over their business as soon as they have said yes to external equity finance. Conflict is always possible, therefore, between founders and investors. For many the experience can be unpleasant. Andrew Palmer told the *Financial Times* in 2004:

> Any entrepreneur raising private equity should keep £100,000 in reserve in case you need to sue your backers. Otherwise you will be dead. They are experts in negotiating and tying up the small print. They will say [an advantageous] clause is needed "just to protect investors", but don't you believe it.

Palmer felt he had reason to be bitter. After a successful launch, New Covent Garden Soup struggled with the management and organisational challenges that came with growth. Its venture-capitalist backers stepped in with the cash to turn it around, initially giving Palmer a second chance to sort things out, but then forcing his removal from the top role in the business, and ultimately from the board.

Growth is hungry for finance, and business founders and owners have to recognise that in return for finance they will need to give away a stake in the business. That stake might earn for the investor the right to a dividend, though dividends are usually paid only by large businesses; many small businesses cannot afford dividends and even their investors would rather see the cash conserved and invested back in the business. The real payday for most equity investors comes when they exit: either by selling their stake, or by an overall sale or float of the business. If they are lucky, equity investors will earn much more from their investment than a bank will from its interest. But the risks are much higher too. Equity investors ride their luck and get rewarded for it. A bank lending money likes to make sure that luck has been eliminated, at least as far as the bank is concerned.

Many entrepreneurs are rightly nervous about bringing institutional equity finance into the business they have founded. They worry about the prospect of seeing an equity investor riding away with a sizable sum of money made at their expense, and about the mismatch between their ambitions and those of the finance house. Most importantly, they recognise that giving shares to an outside investor always means that someone else is able, to a greater or lesser extent, to get involved in where the business is going and how it is run. Many entrepreneurs fight hard against the temptation to take institutional funding, and scrimp and save instead. Some argue that funding a business in its early stages by bootstrapping in many circumstances is healthier and is more likely to foster a business that focuses on building the top line and maintaining healthy margins. But owners and managers who believe that institutional equity finance is right for their businesses should make sure they think about more than just the money. Business owners should look long and hard at the investors as well as the quality of their cash. Can you work with them? Do you like them as people? Do they understand your business? Are they flexible? Do they have something else to add other than money? If these questions are not answered satisfactorily, the owners should walk away; and even if the answers are satisfactory, they should look around for alternatives.

If new money is the difference between potentially growing the business, or not growing it at all, or even going under, there is every reason for equity investors to be welcomed, particularly when they bring ideas, experience and possibly customers (and can resist the temptation to meddle too much in operations). After all, a slice of a big cake is much more interesting than the whole of a cupcake, let alone no cake at all.

Going public

When the shares of a company are available for the general public to buy on a regulated stockmarket, such as the London Stock Exchange or the New York Stock Exchange, the company is said to be listed.

Obtaining a listing for the first time is known as a flotation or an initial public offering (IPO).

Entrepreneurs are often equivocal about going public. Mark Zuckerberg, founder of Facebook, outlined (on Facebook in September 2010) arguments that many entrepreneurs will be familiar with:

> We aren't planning to go public anytime soon. As a company, I think we look at going public differently than many other companies do. For a lot of companies, going public is the end goal and they shoot for and optimize around it. For us, going public isn't a goal in itself; it's just something we'll do when it makes sense for us. Since we compensate people at Facebook with stock and we took investment, I view it as my responsibility to eventually make that stock liquid for people, but that doesn't have to happen in the short term and our primary responsibility is still just to make sure Facebook develops to its full potential.
>
> I tend to think that being private is better for us right now because of some of the big risks we want to take in developing new products ... The experience of managing the company through launching controversial services is tricky, but I can only imagine it would be even more difficult if we had a public stock price bouncing around. There are a lot more new things left to build like the examples I mentioned above, and I'd rather focus on building them than on going public right now.

For founders who stay around after the businesses they founded go public the experience can be traumatic. When promoting her book *Business as Unusual* in 2001, Anita Roddick, founder of Body Shop, said:

> Did flotation work? Well, it gave us money to build manufacturing plants ... Does it work now? I do not think so. [The Body Shop has] lost its soul since floating on the stock market ... it has no place as a cog in the international finance system ... [The Body Shop] is now really a dysfunctional coffin.

Roddick described attempting to take her business private again on at least two occasions, so that she could do business away from the glare of investor scrutiny. Richard Branson cheerfully floated Virgin on the stockmarket but bought it back again in 1998, stating, "Being an entrepreneur and the chairman of a public company just do not mix." Entrepreneurs in the United States have been just as equivocal about taking their own companies public, as Zuckerberg's comments indicate.

Stelios Haji-Iannou's evolving relationship with easyJet is interesting in this regard. When resigning as chairman of easyJet in April 2002, he was quoted in the *Financial Times* as saying:

> *Starting a company requires a very different skill-set from those needed to chair a major plc, and I consider my strengths are in the former. The history of the City is littered with entrepreneurs who held on to their creations for too long, failing to recognise the changing needs of the company.*

It is not recorded whether Haji-Iannou remembered these words when, in a public row with management in November 2008, he argued that the company's growth strategy needed reining back, and a dividend needed paying by 2011. If he did not get his way, he threatened to exercise a right reserved to him: as long as he held more than 25% of the shares, he could appoint two non-executive directors. And as long as he held more than 10%, he retained the right to make himself chairman. The agreement could not be changed "unless approved by a resolution of the board, at which an independent non-executive is in the majority".

The source of Haji-Iannou's unusual power was a "relationship agreement" drafted at the time of easyJet's flotation. To be fair, the document stated that the company should have its own management, and that it should "make decisions for the benefit of shareholders as a whole and independently of the controlling shareholders at all times". But the clauses described above seem to have different implications for the role of the board. In the *Sunday Times* in November 2008 Haji-Iannou was quoted as saying: "I am merely applying my rights under the articles of incorporation of the company to protect my investment." The row continued to simmer through 2009, and in April 2009 easyJet's chairman, Colin Chandler, announced he was stepping down. He was reported in the *Guardian* as saying:

[I am] fed up with the situation of running a board, which is tough. You have got a recession, there are some strong characters on the board and public companies these days are very tough to run.

For his part, Haji-Iannou reportedly described the situation as "a debate, not a dispute". By July 2009, with the airline industry in crisis, the irony was that Haji-Iannou was seen to have won the argument; easyJet scaled back its plans. Some described it as a triumph of the entrepreneur over the money men.

In October 2010, however, Haji-Iannou agreed to give up the right to make boardroom appointments and allowed easyJet to keep its name. He signed a new licence agreement allowing the airline to enter branding agreements with other firms to sell things like insurance, hotels or car hire, even if this meant competing directly with easyGroup. The deal also made it easier for easyJet to lease planes from other firms to meet any extra demand, which had previously required easyGroup's consent. Other terms prohibited him from starting up a rival airline for five years and forced him to abide by "public communication protocols". In return, he received 0.25% of easyJet's turnover for up to 50 years, fixed at £3.9m ($6.25m) in the first year and £4.95m ($7.9m) the next, plus another £300,000 ($480,000) annually. The new chief executive, Carolyn McCall, said: "It gives us more freedom to operate and much greater clarity."

That many founders find the experience of listing so uncomfortable shows just how big a transition it is. Indeed, a listing on a stockmarket is a crucial change in the history of a business, marking the separation of ownership from management. What should owner-managers think about when considering listing their businesses?

Positives

- It gives companies another important tool for financing business expansion and corporate acquisitions. Instead of paying cash to the shareholders of a target company, a company can offer its shares. It also makes it easier to reduce gearing.
- It is easier to remunerate staff using options or shares. If there is a ready market for the shares, individuals can convert their holdings into cash, subject to scheme rules.

- Listed companies and their directors are more highly respected than private businesses by the media, potential employees, customers and creditors.

Negatives

- Businesses that succeed on the markets must be confident that they can satisfy market expectations of stability and long-term growth; the markets, and the analysts that interpret and comment on them, do not like surprises. Usually businesses can be confident of such stability only once they have achieved a certain level of maturity; this partly explains why bigger companies often fare better on the markets than smaller ones.

- Financial markets are notoriously short-termist. They respond to the financial reporting cycles dictated by market regulation and company law, which for listed companies means not just the annual financial statements, but also interim and quarterly announcements. Owner-managers accustomed to taking a longer-term view often struggle with the short-term preoccupations of the markets. This was the case with Virgin, which bought back its shares shortly after listing. Branson said that the business's long-term goals were being compromised. However, the Virgin empire has always been opaque, despite the warm and ostensibly open personality of its founder (who dislikes the public glare on his rather secret way of doing business). Opacity does not sit well with a listing on a regulated stockmarket.

- The process is time consuming and expensive, and will affect day-to-day business management.

- Maintaining a listing is expensive.

- There will be greater public scrutiny of directors' and management's actions and a more onerous set of regulations. Many have been lured by the glory an IPO is perceived to bestow on a company's directors, without appreciating the change of role that goes with it. Many former owner-managers/ CEOs of newly listed businesses moan about how much time they have to invest in investor relations and answering analysts' questions.

- A listed company is no longer in control of its own destiny and can be subject to hostile takeover, particularly if its shares fail to perform.

- A listing provides the current owners with an opportunity to realise part of their investment, but it is not in itself an exit for the owners.

- A flotation is easier to achieve when the markets are doing well than when they are doing badly. In 2009, the world's stockmarkets virtually shut up shop for new entrants. Lastminute.com famously got its flotation away days before the dotcom bubble burst. Other arguably more robust business propositions missed the opportunity, and some wasted a lot of management time and cost in preparation.

- A listed company is subject to the vagaries of the market. Share prices go down as well as up. The advisers of a company seeking to offer its shares on the market usually try to pitch the price at a level that allows the early investors a small increase in value. But the future for a share, particularly a new share, can be difficult to predict, and luck seems to have as much of an influence as the skills of management and their advisers. Unfortunately, many of the positives associated with having listed shares depend on the market perceiving those shares to be attractive. Of course, a company will pay the costs of a listing regardless.

A demanding process

Different markets demand different processes for flotation or IPO. The following briefly reflects what is typically involved.

A flotation takes time. The process itself is unlikely to take less than six months and could well take up to a year. And the business needs to be groomed for the market – if it wants to succeed, it needs to look the part before it gets there. In particular, its board, management team and governance processes need to be fit for purpose. As a minimum this might require changing some individuals at the top of the company;

the recruitment of new non-executive directors; different approaches to public relations, brand management and customer care; and ensuring that internal accounting systems are able to cope with the new demands that will be made. Because private companies enjoy a less onerous regulatory environment, there might well be skeletons that need shaking out of the cupboards. Senior managers and directors will have to accept and act in accordance with new standards of behaviour. Many find this hard. Grooming a company can easily add another year to the preparation process, if not longer.

As well as sorting out its own house, a company interested in floating needs to recruit new teams of advisers. It will need a sponsor to co-ordinate its entry to the market. It may also need a corporate broker, though sometimes this can be the same firm as the sponsor. It will need reporting accountants, lawyers and tax advisers, as well as experienced public relations advisers. Long-standing corporate advisers might need to be changed. Lawyers and accountants who have successfully guided the business through the entrepreneurial early years, venture capital and private equity, might not have the skills and experience required for listing. None of these will come cheap.

There are different ways in which a company can go public. At one end of the scale is a (relatively) cheap and simple introduction to the market, raising no new money. A placing, in which shares are offered for sale to institutions selectively, might be in a company's best interests. At the other end of the scale is a public offer, in which both institutions and private individuals are invited to subscribe. A company's advisers will help identify the best route.

Whatever method of listing it chooses, the company and its advisers have to prepare a prospectus or listing particulars, as appropriate. This sets out all the information that has to be made public to investors under the listing rules. It also acts as an important piece of PR, providing a description of the business, its areas of activity and its prospects. The period from the preparation of the accountants' report on the company to the start of dealing on the main market is often around 24 weeks, although it can be less. The stages making up this period will depend on the route selected for flotation. Although a company looking for an introduction has to follow through the full due diligence and disclosure process, including the preparation of listing particulars, it probably will not need to conduct investor road shows. A flotation involving an offer for subscription to the public is a much bigger project. As well as the full due diligence and disclosure process, including the preparation of a prospectus, the company will probably have to participate in various marketing activities, including road shows, alongside the regulatory and disclosure duties.

While all this is going on, the company's directors will be having meetings with officials from the stock exchange to discuss the business and look at ways in which the stock exchange can help in developing an active trading market following admission. It is easy to forget that a listing is the start of something, not an end in itself. The company's lawyers will also be conducting the verification process, a painstaking task involving the confirmation of every statement or claim in each document. Precise valuations of the company's assets are produced. This often requires the involvement of yet more advisers and people such as actuaries and surveyors. Verification of directors' particulars often requires the directors to dig into their personal and professional records.

One of the most important decisions is the price put on the company's share. The sponsor and broker will want a realistic price that the market will find attractive, whereas the company will naturally wish to raise as much money as possible. If underwriters are involved, their views must be taken into account too, as they will be exposed if the shares are not taken up. With good reason the final decision is left as late as possible, largely because market conditions can change overnight. Indeed, the price is often the last thing to go into the prospectus. In the worst-case scenario, a listing might have to be pulled in the event of a market collapse, which would leave the company with advisers' fees to pay and no listing to show for it.

7   People and growth

PEOPLE ARE THE MOST IMPORTANT resource in any business, the least understood and often the least well used. Scott Adams's Dilbert notes that for most businesses "money" is the most important asset, with "people coming much lower down the list – after carbon paper". But as has already been noted, investors invest in people, not businesses, so in this instance Dilbert, of course, got it wrong.

The problem is that people can be emotional, unpredictable and awkward. Furthermore, the right people can be difficult to hire and the wrong ones difficult to fire. However, a business that pays attention to people and manages them intelligently will find growth easier to achieve and sustain.

Recruitment

A business that is growing is a business that is recruiting. It is also one that needs in particular to be mindful of the skills that are needed in the next stage of the business's evolution as well as those it needs now. It should also take care when recruiting the next generation of management not to overpromise and therefore disappoint.

Integrating new members of staff into a growing business can also be difficult, especially when they are replacing staff members who have been fired or were liked, or their appointment involves an adjustment to the roles of current staff, as is often the case in a changing, growing business, in which recruitment is being used as a catalyst for change. Existing employees tend to view changes of any kind with suspicion. (See Chapter 4.)

Recruiting staff from outside also has an inflationary impact on staff costs. Unless they happen to find themselves on the job market for reasons not of their own making, good recruits will need reasons to leave their current employers. Some will be prepared to move to secure better long-term opportunities, but in other instances a salary increase will be necessary to secure the move – and this may cause problems if and when their new colleagues find out.

Recruitment is both a science and an art and requires a serious commitment of management time, thought and effort, even when a professional recruitment firm is being used. Businesses often find it difficult to justify using a third-party organisation to assist with recruitment. For junior-level posts, it is often cost effective for a business to do the work itself, particularly with the internet offering many advertising options. For senior-level posts, however, advisers can help. Good advisers add a measure of objectivity. They can structure a selection process that gives the business the best chance of finding the right candidate, minimising the subjective elements in what will always remain a demanding exercise fraught with personal judgments. Advisers also provide an ear for candidates. Many good candidates are wary of applying directly to a company but are willing to approach an intermediary, confident of being able to have exploratory discussions while retaining confidentiality. A company that seeks to recruit directly to senior positions without using advisers runs the risk of not attracting some candidates with real potential.

Getting the best from people

Growth demands change from the business and development on the part of key people within it. The systems necessary to do this effectively should provide personal goals and targets for employees in the context of career plans that are aligned with the plans for the business. Personal achievement should be assessed against these targets and actions recommended; these should be documented and reviewed later against a revised set of targets. In other words, a growing business needs effective staff appraisal systems that complement its growth plans.

Performance management and appraisal

Big businesses nowadays are comfortable with formal appraisal mechanisms for staff. Most small businesses deal with staff appraisal at best informally, at worst not at all. Far too many rely on a pay review (or lack of it) to pass on the good or bad news, leave the communication of detail to osmosis, assume that anyone who makes a mistake is not worth employing anyway, and trust the "X-factor" and "gut feeling" as substitutes for the analysis of competency and capability. Even the smallest businesses benefit from formal appraisal of staff. The system need not be complicated; it should include a robust discussion about an individual's performance, an opportunity to discuss the individual's future in the context of the organisation's future, an agreed action plan and some form of formal record of the process.

As an organisation gets bigger and the points of contact for individual staff become more diverse, some form of feedback or comment from different parts of the organisation on an individual's performance can be useful. Some organisations invest in complicated, computer-based "360-degree" assessment systems – in which individuals score each other using pre-set competency questionnaires – which churn out sophisticated aggregate reports for the organisation and for each individual. Such systems can be expensive. They can also be inflexible and difficult to adjust for the change that inevitably comes with growth. Lastly, and most importantly, they depend for their effectiveness on participants submitting truthful feedback. If you put rubbish in, you will only get rubbish out.

Simplicity is always best in a growing, changing business. At the other end of the scale are invitations to a select group of individuals to produce "three up, three down" reports on each other. Each individual is required to identify and note three strengths and three development needs for the colleague in question. Information such as this, collected from two or three individuals with whom the appraisee has worked during the period under review, greatly enhances an appraisal discussion – and at little expense.

Another common form of performance management system is the balanced scorecard methodology developed by American academics and consultants Robert Kaplan and David Norton in the 1990s. This provides a mechanism for adding strategic non-financial performance measures to traditional financial measures when planning for and assessing the achievement of corporate strategic goals. The framework suggests how first departmental targets and measures, and then individuals' personal targets, might be drafted to reinforce corporate strategies. Corporate strategy is thus translated into detailed actions for individual members of staff. Kaplan and Norton describe their framework as follows:[18]

> *The balanced scorecard retains traditional financial measures. But financial measures tell the story of past events, an adequate story for industrial age companies for which investments in long-term capabilities and customer relationships were not critical for success. These financial measures are inadequate, however, for guiding and evaluating the journey that information age companies must make to create future value through investment in customers, suppliers, employees, processes, technology, and innovation.*

It is easy to see why this mechanism has been popular with large corporations interested in focusing the efforts of all staff on achieving growth.

Some individuals take the view that appraisals are processes only for junior staff. This is not true. Board directors of major corporations benefit as much from regular, formal appraisal as junior assistants. Indeed, the Corporate Governance Code for listed companies in the UK requires that the board should undertake a formal and rigorous annual valuation of its own performance and that of its committees and individual directors. The code also stipulates that the review of the boards of FTSE 350 companies should be externally facilitated every three years.

Training and development

As well as being appraised, individuals should be trained. The case for training staff is strong in any business. Business leaders who take the view that training is too expensive should consider the potential costs (in terms of failing to keep up with the times or the competition as well as the everyday needs of the business) of not training their staff. In a growing business the case is particularly strong because of the change that is part and parcel of growth; anyone whose role is changing is likely to need assistance in acquiring the skills that will be needed to carry it out well. One serial entrepreneur observes that senior managers newly recruited to fast-growth businesses should accept that their new role will have changed even between the time they accept the job and the day they start it.

The most senior individuals in the biggest businesses also need to refresh their skills and learn new ones. Corporate governance codes propose as good practice that the chairman should regularly review and agree with each director their training and development needs.

Training and development can only go so far. Senior managers in growing businesses should recognise the point when the needs of the business grow beyond the capabilities of staff. Again, what is true for junior staff is also true for senior directors. One experienced executive observed that a business needed to change its finance director when it reached a turnover of £7m, £17m and £70m. The numbers may be wrong but the sentiment is correct. For many it is not so much capabilities that are exceeded but desires. Many managers want to work only in small or early-stage businesses. When the business has firmly established itself and grown and they feel their job has been done and is less interesting, it is time to move on. Another factor commonly forgotten in the context of business evolution is the age of members of the management team. Individuals change as they grow older, and so do their priorities, desires and expectations. Increasingly, retirement is not really the issue, though it is undoubtedly important to acknowledge personal plans to withdraw from the business. What is more important is to ensure that an individual's changing priorities are acknowledged and reconciled with development and business plans.

To nurture, to retain, or to …

Businesses with ambitions to grow often find themselves torn between two human resources strategies. The first is an "up-or-out" strategy. The most valuable staff are expected to progress along defined career paths according to timescales. Failure to progress in effect means their career with that particular organisation is over, and it is only a matter of when they will leave. Organisations adopting this strategy foster competitive organisational cultures. They depend on senior posts in the organisation being sufficiently attractive to stoke competition among junior staff.

Large professional services organisations – lawyers, management consultancies and banks – typically adopt this type of strategy. It appears to be wasteful; in an up-or-out organisation there are bound to be capable individuals who leave because they feel they are unlikely to win the promotion that might have kept them. How can such a strategy be reconciled with the pressures of growth, one of the barriers to which is the capability and capacity of senior management? Such organisations argue that staff who make the grade will make their own business, and that an up-or-out culture is an effective way of reconciling human resources and business needs. They also argue that the strategy makes for clean, efficient people-management, with far less attention paid to remuneration strategy, for example as a lever for change. As the HR director at an international consulting firm observed:

We do not need to pay bonuses here: if you're good enough to work for us you'll be well paid; if you're not good enough you will not get paid less, you will not work for us at all.

The alternative strategy is one in which an organisation works harder at retaining staff, trying to find the right level for everyone. Under up-or-out, middle-ranking positions are held by individuals who are on the way to the top or on the way out. Under the alternative strategy, middle-ranking positions may be held by individuals moving far more slowly through the organisation, or not moving at all. It is easier to reconcile such an approach with the inevitable shortage of capable senior staff in a growing organisation. However, such a strategy puts more pressure on performance management systems: there is not much difference between individuals finding their own level and the organisation tolerating lower standards.

Regardless of the strategy adopted, when staff leave their departure should be handled as constructively as possible so that they are likely to represent the organisation well to the outside world. Organisations with up-or-out strategies can have just as effective alumni programmes as firms with softer approaches. Alumni from management consultancy McKinsey hold roles across industry, commerce and government. Most will be pleased to acknowledge their time at McKinsey, even though many were in effect asked to leave. Former staff are among the most powerful and credible ambassadors any business can have. Big businesses often invest in alumni management programmes. Small businesses cannot do this, but time, energy and money invested in ensuring that staff who are leaving are looked after, and kept in contact with, will pay dividends.

Remuneration

The remuneration of staff is a difficult issue in any business. In a growing business or one ambitious for growth, it is often even more difficult. In growing businesses cash is often under pressure, so there is less available for paying staff. Smaller businesses have fewer resources than bigger businesses anyway, but if they wish to grow they need to attract and retain people with the qualities and experience necessary to take the business to the next stage of its evolution. Again, this will not come cheap.

Bonus considerations

Many new and ambitious businesses favour including some form of performance-related or deferred remuneration element. If a business cannot afford to pay good money now it can at least guarantee that if targets are met the individuals responsible for the success will be rewarded in due course. Mechanisms for delivering performance-related or deferred rewards include bonus and equity schemes (including share options). Both can be powerful tools for motivating staff, but they come with health warnings.

Most bonus schemes are introduced with too little thought, and so the following should be borne in mind:

- A good bonus scheme rewards employees for achieving predetermined targets. Defining such targets for a growing business can be difficult (see Chapter 5).

- Staff should perceive bonus schemes as being fair. But it can be difficult to determine which staff members have been responsible for what, and the allocation of bonuses at the end of a period can be divisive. Managers seeking to pick and choose between staff will have their judgments questioned. However, those who take the view that everyone contributed so all should benefit may find that staff think some of their number have been unfairly rewarded for riding on the backs of others.

- It is difficult to capture everything that matters in a set of performance measures that can then be tied to a bonus scheme. There is a trade-off between the wish to capture the complexity of reality and the need to design a scheme that is simple enough for staff to understand and that will influence change. If there are too many variables, staff will find it difficult to identify clearly what they need to do to achieve their bonuses, and therefore may not bother to make the effort the bonus scheme seeks to encourage. No more than three variables will ensure the clearest link between remuneration and performance. However, performance is rarely a matter of successfully delivering two or three variables, so such a system is likely to distort staff behaviour in some way. Simple systems that distort behaviour can be used to influence change; sophisticated systems that attempt to capture the complexity of a job will be better than simple ones at sharing the spoils fairly, but they will be less help when managing change.

- Employees are always cleverer than the bonus schemes designed to motivate them, no matter how sophisticated the schemes. Bonus schemes should be thought of as short-term only. If they are left in place for too long staff will find the loopholes, and the negative effects of the system will outweigh the positive.

- Staff do not react to bonus schemes in the same way. This can come as a surprise to managers. It may be attractive to managers to be able to link remuneration to future performance, but many staff would rather settle for a guaranteed higher income now than the prospect that it could, if all goes well, turn out to be much higher in the end. As one HR director observed: too many bonus schemes are just an excuse for not paying people properly to start with.

■ Bonuses are best at providing short-term reward for short-term performance. If the behaviours sought have long-term rather than short-term consequences, equity-based rewards should be considered.

Options and other equity-based incentives

Equity-based incentives, including share options, have several advantages for growing businesses. They defer the payout of cash and are thus easier to align with long-term growth plans. They can be used to tie employees to the business: if they leave early, they may lose their rights to benefit from the scheme. Usually the source of the cash will be outside the business, coming from a future acquirer of the company's shares. The use of equity as a reward can also help engender a sense of ownership. However, such schemes are not without drawbacks:

■ Equity and option schemes can be complicated and expensive to establish in terms of advisers' fees, in particular, as well as management time and effort – and these are costs that cannot be deferred. Businesses considering using such schemes should not cut corners. Professional advice should be taken to ensure documentation is in place to cover as many future eventualities as possible. This may include shareholder agreements and changes to employment terms and conditions. The costs of getting it wrong can be much more expensive than the set-up costs. Shareholder disputes can tear a company apart.

■ In many jurisdictions equity and option schemes are viewed favourably by the authorities, particularly in the case of small companies, and are subject to advantageous tax schemes. Indeed, tax, for both the individuals and the company, is a particular and ever-changing complication that needs to be taken into account when introducing equity or option schemes. But tax should be thought of as the cart not the horse. Tax schemes can have the effect of encouraging management to focus on saving tax rather than more strategic business imperatives. What seemed like a good idea when the scheme was established can turn into a poisoned pill if it needs to be unwound for whatever unforeseen reason.

■ In start-ups there are important issues to consider when deciding how much equity to give to whom. Many founding teams fudge the issue and give equal shares. Four friends with 25% each of the equity might seem fair in theory, but the result might be organisational stalemate after the four have fallen out and old friends start taking sides and voting accordingly. Besides, an equal allocation of equity presumes an equal contribution from everyone. This is rarely the case. When assessing contribution, team members should focus on capital contribution. Capital often takes the form of cash to finance the venture, but it can also take other forms – intellectual capital, for example.

■ Neither equity nor options mean much if the holder cannot see a way of turning them into cash. For public companies whose shares are quoted on the stockmarket there is no problem, but most growing businesses are not in this position. For private companies there is not a ready market for their shares, so schemes in such companies work best when there is a clear exit route that reinforces the overall business objectives. Classic exit routes include floating the business (quoting its shares on the stockmarket) or a trade sale (selling the business to another business). In the absence of an exit route, equity and options are far less effective as incentives.

■ Scheme members in listed companies are more excited about equity or options when stockmarkets are doing well than when they are doing badly. When share prices are going down, their owners have reason for being doubly demoralised. A decision to "rebase" an option that is worthless because the share price has fallen below the exercise price on the option often results in ordinary stockholders crying foul.

■ As with bonuses, equity and option schemes are often implemented by entrepreneurs who are motivated by holding equity in the businesses they have founded. Many of the next generation of management may not be interested in such schemes, though they may be reluctant to admit this in a recruitment interview. Conversely, for those genuinely interested in the roller-coaster ride of a fast-growth start-up, equity participation may be just what they want. Business founders rightly nervous about giving equity to an untested member of the team should make sure it is not given on appointment but only after, say, the satisfactory completion of a probation period.

Making it a team effort

As with most other aspects of management, growing a business, whether it is new and small or large and established, is very much a team activity. "Without [Sinclair Beecham] it wouldn't work; without me it wouldn't be there," noted Julian Metcalfe of the joint contributions he and his fellow founder made to Pret a Manger. Research consistently shows that businesses founded by teams grow further and faster than businesses founded by individuals.

Team is perhaps too scientific a term for what, in a start-up, is often little more than a group of friends. Such teams need to ensure that their business is set up in such a way that it stands the best chance of surviving a failure in the friendship, so often the consequence of even a successful business venture between friends. John D. Rockefeller, according to a 1998 biography by Ronald Chernow, was fond of quoting his partner Henry Morrison Flagler's dictum that a friendship based on business is superior to a business based on friendship.

In their book, *The Wisdom of Teams,* Jon Katzenbach and Douglas Smith argue that, in businesses big and small, good teams do not just happen.[19] Without investment in team construction and management, the group will not even add up to the sum of its parts. But with such an investment, the parts may combine to become a high-performance team delivering far in excess of the sum of the individual contributions.

Out of the wealth of thinking that has gone into the management of teams, the following points are worth noting by a team with responsibility for growing the business.

Leadership

The role of team leader should be defined and allocated. In young businesses, particularly those founded by groups of friends, there is often a lack of clarity about the role of the leader. The leader of an established business is usually the CEO or managing director, who runs the business through the management team he or she is responsible for building and leading. In bigger businesses the role is often split between the chairman and the CEO, with the former responsible for the board and holding the CEO to account for the running of the business.

Complementary strengths and capabilities

Good teams include individuals with different strengths and capabilities; those who are similar often tread on each other's toes. Team-building methodologies give different labels to the different roles, often identifying the various personality types most likely to succeed in them. Meredith Belbin, an authority on teams, refers to the plant (the creative problem solver), the resource investigator (the enthusiastic opportunity explorer), the co-ordinator (the chairperson), the shaper (thriving on pressure and focusing the team's attention on its goals), the monitor-evaluator (calmly reviewing and assessing options), the implementer (turning ideas into action), the teamworker (the doer who avoids friction and gets things done) and the specialist (providing technical know-how for the task in hand). None of these labels are used around real boardroom tables, but the notion that there are different types of activity within a team, and different types of people required to do them, is often ignored.

In many businesses the role of team members is to agree with the boss, and the best way of guaranteeing advancement is to take the boss as a role model. The finance director or chief financial officer is often the only person who likes to say "no", but the CEO should be open to challenge from every member of the senior management team, executive and non-executive.

Clear objectives and a disciplined approach

A team will be more effective if it has clear objectives. For a team responsible for growing a business, this means drafting a long-term plan for the business, together with a shorter-term action plan and a budget that are aligned with the long-term plan (see Chapter 4).

Regular management meetings should be documented and agreed actions should be assigned to individuals and followed up. In short, meetings should be disciplined. A good chairman will make sure that all points of view are heard, that unresolved conflicts are identified and addressed, that, where appropriate, individuals are held accountable for their actions and that team members do not fall into false consensus, with bullying or boredom taking the place of judgment and debate.

It is not just the main leadership roles that should be carefully defined. Every member of a team responsible for managing growth should be aware of the scope of their authority and the nature of their expected contribution. Such definition, and the diversity it depends on, is easier in a bigger team than in a smaller one. Big businesses are more likely to be able to afford big teams. In small businesses individuals may have several jobs. Multitasking often extends outside the boardroom. In a family business, for example, an operations director might also be a shareholder, the mother of another board director, the daughter of the company founder (who is also a non-executive) and an influential individual in the local community. That individuals are required to play a variety of roles in many small businesses is often considered to be a strength; a team in which individuals share responsibilities is likely to be more flexible than one in which roles are clearly delineated. This is true, but lack of role definition can hinder accountability, particularly when the team is under pressure and the various bucks that are flying around need to be shared out or specifically allocated.

Discipline is not just about the conduct of individual meetings. Even small businesses can benefit from a business calendar, circulated in advance to the management team or board members, indicating when in the year various matters will be discussed. These might include strategy and business planning, budgeting, pay reviews, shareholder management and governance. In listed businesses, boardroom discipline is governed in great part by corporate governance codes. But smaller businesses need discipline too.

Decision-taking

The easiest decisions to take are those that everyone agrees on, though it is important that all sides of an issue are explored first. Where members of the team disagree a healthy debate should be easier to initiate, and opinions may well change as a consequence. A CEO is likely to be more influential than other members of a management team, but if consensus cannot be achieved, other mechanisms for taking decisions will be needed, and these should have been agreed in advance. Ultimately, of course, a shareholder with a majority of the voting power can force decisions through.

Measuring success

Defined mechanisms for acknowledging and measuring success help team performance. In the case of a senior management team, these include business performance indicators that attempt to capture all aspects of business performance (see Chapter 5), and a dashboard of key performance indicators (KPIs) that focus management's attention on the critical elements of business performance. In the case of a team responsible for implementing growth, the growth plan should include a framework for assessing progress.

Intangible strengths and vulnerabilities

The building of a business involves creating an entity with a distinctive identity separate from the founders. Internally, this identity is a composite of a particular organisational culture and set of values. The external manifestation of this identity in a successful organisation is seen most readily in the brand proposition. Where do these elements come from? An example will help.

David Bruce built his pub business, Bruce's Breweries, the way he wanted, notwithstanding rational and well-meant advice to the contrary from advisers and financiers. Made redundant in 1979 by one of the big brewers several recessions ago, Bruce put his money into a rundown pub in London's Elephant and Castle district. But he did more than give the establishment a good refit. Out went the jukebox even though his bank manager advised him it would bring large amounts of much needed cash every night; Bruce did not like turning up to a pub for a drink and having to shout at his friend over someone else's choice of music. He also put a microbrewery behind the bar and announced his intention to brew his own beer on site. He renamed the pub the Goose and Firkin. It was a great success. Within a few years Bruce was running a chain of pubs in south-east England, each of which brewed on site and none of which had jukeboxes. They all had "and Firkin" in their titles, thus giving rise to a slightly risqué advertising campaign playing on the mispronunciation of "firkin" after a pint or two, which appealed to Bruce's sense of humour.

After nine years Bruce surprised everyone by selling his business to European Leisure in 1988, which in 1991 sold it to Allied Domecq, which in 1999 sold it to Punch Taverns. A couple of years later Punch sold over half the pubs to Bass (now Mitchells & Butlers). After founder owner-manager Bruce had sold it, the business became the concern of a series of teams of professional managers, who worked successfully for a while growing the estate. But before long the character of the pubs changed significantly and the jukeboxes were back. In due course, the microbreweries went and were replaced with higher-margin bought-in real ale. Growth slowed, then stopped. In 2001 Punch announced that the Firkin brand was to be discontinued. Some of the pubs still keep the Firkin name, which has been used by chains in the United States, Canada and elsewhere (with no connection to the original business), but most of the UK pubs have been renamed. Even the original Goose and Firkin is now the Duke of York.

It is easy to conclude that the Firkin story is just about brand building, or a brand that had run its course. Far more important for those interested in growing businesses is that many of the elements of the business Bruce built were derived from his personal preferences, his personality, even his sense of humour – rather than manufactured as a consequence of rational analysis. Indeed, if he had taken the advice of the rationalists at the start, his business might have looked very different. Once Bruce had sold the business it changed quite quickly.

Other companies in similar circumstances have tried to manage such transitions more carefully. When Ben Cohen and Jerry Greenfield sold Ben and Jerry's, the ice cream business they had founded, to Unilever in 2000, many wondered whether the company's culture would change, particularly regarding its participation in global ecological and environmental campaigns. Unilever announced its determination to carry on with the campaigning, even though Cohen and Greenfield had stepped down from management involvement. Although Ben and Jerry's has undoubtedly changed in the years since 2000, Unilever has remained true to its word.

As Bruce's Breweries and Ben and Jerry's show, many of the important intangible elements of organisational cultures, values and brands are derived from the personalities of the founders. However, when a business has grown larger or the founder has sold out, it can be difficult to preserve these elements. At some stage a growing business will almost certainly lose some of the magic that made it special when it was founded. Managers wishing to recapture these elements need to find ways of recreating them. They cannot rely on rational performance management systems and processes. They need to invest in the irrational: in informal as well as formal communication mechanisms, in symbols, in who sits where, in the design of the office environment, in how things are done as well as what is done.

Some businesses attempt to build their organisational culture by identifying the qualities they believe have stood them in good stead in the past. They then look for ways of preserving them through easy-to-use management tools. For many organisations the solution lies in organisational structure, the size of each organisational unit and the autonomy given to it. Entrepreneurship is often identified as a quality that organisations wish to hang on to even as they get bigger and more institutional. In the context of bigger businesses, entrepreneurship is often labelled intrapreneurship, recognising its differences from as well as its similarities to entrepreneurship in smaller businesses. As well as looking at structural solutions, big businesses wishing to rediscover their entrepreneurial roots might also look at corporate venturing (investing in start-ups), joint ventures with other organisations, acquiring businesses further down the growth ladder, or new products and business lines. They might also consider breaking up into smaller businesses, recognising that parts of the business might be worth more to the shareholders than the big organisation it has become.

Other organisations attempt to build their organisational values from the bottom. They might start by inviting employees to identify the organisation's values and then compare and contrast these with their personal values. Attempts can then be made to explore the gaps between the two value sets, and adjust those of the organisation (if considered necessary) through training programmes, brand-awareness programmes and so on. Such exercises – which will be powerful as they are grounded in values that employees hold dear – can be used to influence all aspects of an organisation's behaviour.

Another intangible element that is worth considering when growing a business is best referred to as the unofficial or informal organisation chart. Once they reach a certain size all businesses will have a formal structure (see Chapter 4), but they will also have an informal structure with communication channels and lines of influence that are unlikely to match those implied by the official structure. Wise managers do not try to force such structures into compliance, recognising that they will always exist and that they provide another set of tools for controlling the business. Research shows that informal, word-of-mouth communication from peer to peer is more likely to be believed than an official e-mail from the CEO. As Suzanne Crampton, John Hodge and Jitendra Mishra say in their 1998 article, "The Informal Communication Network: Factors Influencing Grapevine Activity", in *Public Personnel Management*, sophisticated communicators use these informal networks to their advantage, deciding which channels best suit which message.

Manufactured organisational cultures, compared with those organically derived from personality and belief, can be fragile and buckle under pressure – often the time the workforce needs them most.

Organisational identities can be sources of strength when businesses find themselves in difficulty. They can also become part of the problem. Culture can be difficult to change (not least because it is so difficult to talk about). But a failure to change culture is the reason the majority of change initiatives fail to change anything.

8   Different types of growth

THIS CHAPTER EXPLORES different types of growth, including organic growth and growth by association with another organisation through merger, acquisition or some form of joint venture or alliance. It also considers growth by replication, the pressures of different rates of growth, and growth overseas. Companies are often reluctant to explore different types of growth. Laurence Capron, a professor at INSEAD in France, and Will Mitchell, a professor at Fuqua School of Business in the United States, show in their ten-year study of 162 telecommunications companies that only one-third actively use all the methods available to them. Some companies choose to develop almost all resources in-house; others focus on licensing or joint ventures; others favour mergers and acquisitions. Capron and Mitchell argue that their study[20]

> ... demonstrates conclusively that firms using all the resource acquisition methods outperform those with a narrow approach. Specifically, firms acquiring resources in multiple ways are 46% more likely to survive over a five-year period than those relying mainly on alliances, 26% more likely than those focusing on M&A, and 12% more likely than those sticking with internal development.

Organic growth

Many of the issues, pressures and strategies discussed in this book so far have presumed linear, organic growth. Organic growth is generated from within or, to put it another way, it is growth that does not rely on an acquisition, merger, or other form of association between two or more organisations.

An examination of the ancestral trees of most of today's organisations shows that pure organic growth is rare. Indeed, big businesses without some history of acquisition somewhere are virtually non-existent. But even among big businesses there are undoubtedly some that are less acquisitive than others, and that have worked hard to develop opportunities and resources in-house rather than seeking to acquire them readymade. Apple is an example of such a business, although in 2010 observers commented that it was showing signs of switching to a more acquisition-based strategy.

Companies that choose not to acquire put a lot of faith in their ability to generate ideas, markets, businesses, people and other resources internally. They run the risk of becoming stale, and if they are ambitious for growth they need to find ways of replicating the stimuli and injections of fresh ideas from outside that an acquisition strategy almost always provides. Such companies need:

- corporate planning processes designed in such a way as to challenge existing thinking continuously;
- corporate radar that is tuned in to changes in the market and industry;
- new staff who are rigorously debriefed shortly after arrival for any insight they might have about changes outside;
- customer intelligence programmes that are sensitive to customer feedback.

Data alone are not enough. Managers should have the capability and willingness to interpret the data and adapt business strategy accordingly, which can be difficult if they are responsible for originating the strategy in the first place. One way big businesses keep their managers fresh is by rotating them regularly through different parts of the company – different business streams and job roles as well as different geographical locations. Businesses without the scale to rotate management internally may need to consider recruiting new staff from outside, adopting an up-or-out promotion strategy with regard to current staff.

Growth by acquisition

Growth by acquisition is often illusory. A simple acquisition for cash does not even make an organisation bigger; it converts the cash of one organisation into the assets of another. Even when new shares are issued, assuming the price paid is fair, an acquisition will just result in two and two equalling four. Given that an acquisition consumes management time and attention – both before the event to negotiate the deal and afterwards to make it work – in the short term at least the net result will show two and two making less than four. Growth by acquisition is only really achieved if in a reasonable time frame the result is more than four. But acquisitions are notorious for their inability to deliver the value intended to shareholders. Many are funded partly by fresh injections of capital, in the form of debt or from existing or new shareholders, but even this is no guarantee that growth will be secured. Indeed, research shows that over the longer term only 50% of acquisitions or mergers achieve the financial targets envisaged.

David Harding and Sam Rovit, partners at Bain & Co, have suggested that it can be misguided to think in terms of growth objectives when looking to acquire:[21]

> The primary purpose of mergers and acquisitions is not to grow big fast, although that may be the result, but for companies to do what they do better.

Before exploring an acquisition or a merger, they encourage management to focus on the source of each company's competitive advantage. A successful acquisition should be used either to strengthen that advantage or to transform a company's advantage, for example when the industry has changed and the company has struggled to catch up. Too many deals, they argue, fail because they attempt to transform fundamentally weak business models, or they are entered into in pursuit of growth for its own sake, or they are a consequence of hubris rather than strategy.

In what ways might an acquisition add up to more than the sum of its parts?

Under-valued companies

The most promising acquisition opportunities are those available cheaply. Acquisitions of under-valued companies are often driven by the circumstances of the vendor, who for various reasons might be obliged to sell. A compulsory sale, for whatever reason, is likely to put downward pressure on the sale price of a company, but it also often brings to the market a business that is otherwise strong. Thomas Cook Global Financial Services was put up for sale in 2000 when its majority shareholder, Preussag, acquired the UK's largest travel business, Thomson Travel. The reason for the sale was that Preussag knew that if it pursued its interest in Thomson Travel, the European competition authorities would force it to sell its interest in Thomas Cook's financial services business. Furthermore, one of Thomas Cook's other significant shareholders, Westdeutsche Landesbank, would also be obliged to sell its stake because of its close association with Preussag. And so the disposal was in effect a forced sale and had little to do with the underlying quality of the business, which was eventually acquired by Travelex.

Shareholders might be obliged to sell when a succeeding generation of a family-owned company is not interested in or capable of owning or running the business. Businesses funded by private equity may be sold as shareholders, particularly financial stakeholders, seek to realise some gain. An IPO is another way for a financial stakeholder to exit, but for owner-managers, a sale is often cleaner and more effective; senior managers are more likely to be tied into the company after an IPO. For most founding entrepreneurs, with or without external financial investment, who are excited by and skilled at early business growth, the question is not whether to exit but when is the right time to sell.

Businesses might be put up for sale quickly if the shareholders are under pressure to raise cash. Again, this might be a consequence of another transaction. The new owners of a group might finance their recent acquisition of the bits of the business they want by selling some of the others. A business that is performing badly might be put up for sale because its existing shareholders are unable to make the investments required to turn it around; a distressed sale such as this might well present a good-value opportunity to a purchaser. As a rule, when seeking to make an acquisition, a purchaser should always consider the motivation of the vendor.

A business available only for its full value might still present opportunities for the purchaser if there are strategic benefits to be derived from the acquisition. A trade buyer from the same industry as the business for sale might be able to achieve synergies or cost savings by rationalising duplicate activities after making the acquisition. Trade buyers often offer the highest prices for a business for sale for this reason, combined with their ability to take advantage of existing industry knowledge and expertise.

Injecting new ideas and talent

The strategic benefits of acquisition can be derived from differences as well as similarities between acquirers and their targets. As noted in Chapter 3, Larry Greiner suggests when commenting on his own growth model that in the later stages of a company's evolution in particular further growth might well be dependent on what he calls "extra organisational solutions". An acquisition is often used as a way of injecting new ideas and talent. A recruitment campaign might succeed in recruiting a handful of new managers, but an acquisition might bring in hundreds or thousands, as well as new ways of doing business, business systems, brands, patents, and research and development capabilities. Exposure to such a sudden dose of high-voltage intellectual capital might have a transformative effect on the business of the acquirer, assuming that the businesses can be integrated and the differences between the two turned to positive advantage. An acquisition might also provide a shortcut to new markets, or new customers or geographical areas. An acquisition might be seen as a route to achieving critical mass more quickly than would be the case otherwise, bringing the stability, security and credibility of being bigger.

A study conducted by Ashridge Management College in the UK demonstrates another way of ensuring that an acquisition yields significant value to new shareholders. Published in 2004 by Anthony Mitchell and Simon Hill, it seeks to understand perceptions of the differences between successful and unsuccessful mergers and

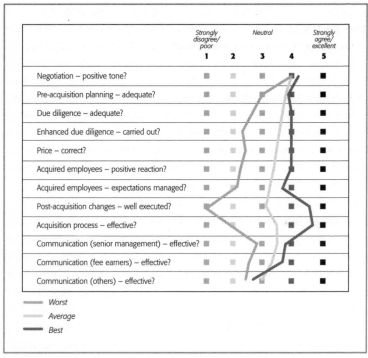

	Strongly disagree/ poor	Neutral			Strongly agree/ excellent
	1	**2**	**3**	**4**	**5**
Negotiation – positive tone?	■	■	■	■	■
Pre-acquisition planning – adequate?	■	■	■	■	■
Due diligence – adequate?	■	■	■	■	■
Enhanced due diligence – carried out?	■	■	■	■	■
Price – correct?	■	■	■	■	■
Acquired employees – positive reaction?	■	■	■	■	■
Acquired employees – expectations managed?	■	■	■	■	■
Post-acquisition changes – well executed?	■	■	■	■	■
Acquisition process – effective?	■	■	■	■	■
Communication (senior management) – effective?	■	■	■	■	■
Communication (fee earners) – effective?	■	■	■	■	■
Communication (others) – effective?	■	■	■	■	■

━━━ *Worst*

━━━ *Average*

━━━ *Best*

Source: Mitchell, A. & Hill, S., "The Great Mergers and Acquisitions Gamble", *The Ashridge Journal 360°*, autumn 2004

FIG 8.1 Process drivers: the best and worst transactions

acquisitions in the marketing communications sector. Figure 8.1 shows that the most significant difference between successful and unsuccessful deals is perceived to be related to the ability to execute change after the acquisition has been completed. Too many acquirers pay little attention to post-acquisition integration. Pursuing the deal has always been perceived as more exciting than managing its implications, but success and its attendant growth depend on successful integration. Integration always springs surprises because, notwithstanding good intentions, acquirers only really get to see what they have bought after completion. Successful integration requires a focus on systems, policies, terms of business, client and customer relationships – there will be differences of approach everywhere. Above all, it requires careful management of people. Members of both acquired and acquiring teams will be suspicious of each other; earning trust will take time. There are bound to be casualties, not all of them looked for.

Some acquirers do not intend to get involved in the management of their new acquisitions, preferring to run them in a "hands-off" way. The terms "hands-off" and "hands-on" imply a black-and-white distinction that does not reflect reality. When one company buys another some form of involvement should be taken for granted, otherwise there is little reason for acquiring the company in the first place. The shareholders of a listed company might complain that if they had wanted to make an investment in the acquired company, they would not have needed the management of the acquiring company to take the decision for them, and perhaps a better use could have been made of the acquiring company's resources. Similarly, "business as usual" claims made by the managers of the acquired company should be taken with a pinch of salt. At the very least the managers will have new owners to answer to; if the managers themselves were also among the shareholders who have sold out, they may well have a reasonable amount of cash, in which case they may find their motivation for day-to-day management of the business under new ownership changing.

In some situations an "earn-out" will be agreed, under which some or all of the consideration is either deferred pending the acquired business achieving targets or based on a variable performance formula negotiated as part of the deal. In theory, such arrangements allow acquirers to mitigate some of the risks associated with the acquisition. However, earn-outs are also sources of potential conflict, especially when the old owner-managers are still involved in the management of the newly acquired subsidiary. It is difficult, for example, for the new owners to step in and influence the direction of their new business; the old owners (if still the current managers) may claim that such interference will prevent them from delivering the numbers they believe are possible and on which some of the consideration is determined.

Management buy-outs

A management buy-out (MBO) is a particular type of acquisition that can provide a platform for future growth for a company. In an MBO, the shareholders sell the company to the existing managers. Typically, the managers will need external finance to finance the transaction, so an MBO will share the characteristics of a venture capital investment (see Chapter 6): rapid growth potential; the potential to get very big; and a definable exit for the financial investors within a time frame that is consistent with the objectives of the fund. An MBO will also share many of the same tensions, in particular between the financial investors and the managers. However, it should mark a significant improvement in the growth prospects of a business or it should not happen in the first place. An MBO should indicate the transfer of control of a business to a team with a greater appetite for growth, driven in no small part by the need to satisfy the demands of the financiers. Managers involved in an MBO do not always recognise what they have chosen to take on – particularly the implications of taking on external finance.

It is common for a management team buying a company to need additional management as well as financial resources. A company bought by a combination of current and new management is sometimes called a BIMBO (buy-in management buy-out). Financiers and advisers with a penchant for acronyms have come up with other variants on the MBO label that reflect the nuances of particular situations.

Only a minority of businesses are suitable for an MBO (or its variants), and an MBO will not be possible in all of those that are suitable. Companies often prohibit MBOs for parts or the whole of the business, with good reason. Managers who are contemplating buying the company they are working for have significant conflicts of interest that might lead them to act against the interests of the current shareholders. For example, they might be tempted to run the business down so as to benefit from a cheaper purchase price when it is time to buy. Furthermore, an MBO, just like any other transaction, demands a huge amount of time and effort, which might be considered by the current shareholders to be better directed at managing the business. So managers dreaming of an MBO need to tread carefully.

Growth by merger

A merger is when two businesses are dissolved into each other. In legal terms, a merger suggests the creation of a new, third business, into which the assets of the two merging businesses are transferred. But, in reality, even when a merger is intended, the transaction is often effected by way of an acquisition, with one organisation paying the shareholders of another for its assets. It is hardly surprising that mergers and acquisitions are often confused, especially when many deals are presented as mergers even though the parties involved intend one partner to be dominant. Indeed, cynics will argue that one partner in a merger is always dominant even when the intention is otherwise. A merger in the true sense, however, is a process in which the end result is an organisation that takes the best of the combining companies and creates something that can generate more than the two could produce separately. Unfortunately, relatively few mergers do.

Big, multi-stakeholder businesses such as listed companies or large professional partnerships are most likely to attempt mergers. Organisations in which individuals or small groups of individuals are dominant find mergers difficult to pull off as, despite good intentions, it is difficult to reconcile the personal aspirations of powerful individuals with the aggregate interests of the newly merged organisation. Even for big businesses a true merger is more difficult to pull off than a successful acquisition. Corus was the product of the merger between Hoogovens, a Dutch company, and British Steel in 1999, aimed at achieving critical mass in the international metals market. It did not deliver. By 2003 Corus's stockmarket valuation had dropped to $230m from $6 billion at the time of the merger. Various reasons were given, including the cultural differences between the merged two organisations and the lack of attention to HR matters on integration; downsizing and cost cutting led to significant labour unrest, which seriously hindered the success of the newly merged company. Corus was bought by Tata, an Indian company, in 2007.

The $182 billion merger of Time Warner and AOL, announced in January 2000, was the largest deal to date and is commonly regarded as the most unsuccessful. Technically this merger was effected by an acquisition – AOL bought Time Warner using stock and debt – but in terms of strategic intent was a merger. Strategically this particular deal made sense as a merger, and so it should have, bearing in mind the amount of brain power from both boardrooms applied to satisfying the business case. The union of the old media world and the new – the creation of a new media organisation with extraordinary reach – had much to commend it. In reality the deal was falling apart even before it was approved by the regulators, by which time the dotcom bubble had burst and the AOL side of the business, the acquiring company, was worth a lot less than it had been when the deal was announced. Economic troubles exacerbated cultural and attitudinal differences between the two sides, and the post-deal integration on which every merger or acquisition depends never took off. By 2010, the combined market value of the two now separated companies was only one-seventh of that of the newly merged firm in 2000.

At the other extreme, ExxonMobil is often cited as an example of one of the most successful mergers – albeit one that joined together companies that, ironically, had originally been created when J.D. Rockefeller senior's Standard Oil was broken up in 1911. The merger successfully achieved cost savings and the integration of two different cultures, though even this transaction was technically a takeover, with, in most instances, Exxon executives appointed to positions senior to their Mobil equivalents.

Other routes to growth

Mergers and acquisitions are not the only ways in which two or more companies can be associated, nor are they the only non-organic platforms for growth.

Minority investments

A minority investment by one company in another can be part of an arrangement intended to provide an impetus to the growth of both. In 2001, McDonald's, a fast-food business, bought 33% of the equity of Pret a Manger, a sandwich retail chain. McDonald's was interested in exploring new avenues for value creation outside its core business. Its investment in Pret a Manger was just one among several it made in successful, up-and-coming fast-food businesses. From Pret's point of view, the investment was accompanied by strategic advice and financial and tactical support for its international expansion plans, facilitating its opening in Japan, in particular. As it turned out, Pret's growth strategy proved to be misjudged; international expansion was more difficult than anticipated and the infrastructure needed to support the scale of investment planned was too expensive. Insufficient attention was paid to the company's core business in the UK, which, in the face of increasingly difficult circumstances, began to lose money. Under new management Pret retrenched, pulling out of Tokyo, cutting back in New York and Hong Kong, and focusing on sorting out the core operation. McDonald's stuck with Pret through the turnaround, only exiting when Pret was sold to Bridgepoint, a private equity firm, for £345m in February 2008, by which time the business was growing well in the UK and prospects were looking good in the United States.

Joint ventures

Companies interested in what they might do with and for each other need not buy or exchange each other's shares; they can just put together some form of joint venture, both as an end in itself and as a means of exploring whether a more formal union between the two companies might be appropriate in due course. Joint ventures range from the very formal to the very informal. There are few legal frameworks to worry about, other than those preventing participants in the same market from colluding in anti-competitive practices. It is down to the parties concerned to determine the nature of the venture and to agree which parts of the arrangement need to be governed by contract, but they are usually built around a contractual arrangement to share in the profits or losses from an arrangement.

A joint venture is normally a vehicle for the delivery of a particular project, resulting in the creation of a venture that has an existence independent of its founders for a predetermined period of time. Unlike a merger or an acquisition, there is no intention on the part of either party to interfere in the management or strategy of the other, except in relation to the joint venture itself. Companies interested in a joint venture should be aware that there are three sets of objectives to be satisfied: those of the joint venture itself and those of each of the joint-venture partners. In other words, joint-venture partners will almost certainly have objectives that they choose not to share with each other. To claim otherwise is to risk underestimating the full value to be derived from a joint venture. For example, it might not achieve the financial targets both parties planned for, but it might provide other benefits, such as giving managers experience that they might not otherwise have had, or enabling the partners to develop intellectual capital that might have taken them much longer on their own, or, indeed, preventing a merger or acquisition that might have proven disastrous to both parties.

Strategic alliances

Joint ventures are generally associated with single, time-specific projects. Strategic alliances are longer term, more general arrangements between companies interested in helping each other create value, thus mitigating the risks associated with an organisation's pursuing a particular course of action on its own. Rosabeth Moss Kanter, a professor at Harvard Business School, likens strategic alliances to modern marriages:[22]

Separate careers, individual cheque books, sometimes different names, but the need to work out the operational overlap around household and offspring.

The formation of a strategic alliance does not necessarily mean the creation of a separate entity to conduct the alliance, though this might happen. Indeed, an alliance is about a relationship not about legal agreements. A strategic alliance will stand a better chance of success if the partners have complementary interests (which does not rule out alliances between potential competitors) and respect each other. But as with joint ventures, parties to an alliance need to be big enough to acknowledge that each party will have its own reasons for being interested in the alliance which the other party cannot necessarily be expected to share or even agree with.

Replication and global expansion

Replication is when a business idea or system is copied and rolled out elsewhere, in another location or maybe another industry. Replication is a strategy that a company might follow in pursuit of its own organic growth. It might choose to replicate in partnership with other organisations, via a joint venture, a franchise arrangement or licensing. Replication is a strategy that new market entrants might follow too. Rather than establish and grow a new concept, an entrepreneur might copy another company's idea, with or without the support or consent of that company.

When expanding overseas it can be useful to work with business partners even when seeking to replicate a proven model. Pret a Manger's attempt to enter the Tokyo market was via a joint venture with its minority shareholder McDonald's. Although eventually unsuccessful, Pret could not have contemplated the venture without the knowledge and experience of McDonald's. Expansion into some territories is prohibited unless done in conjunction with a local partner, and even where it is permitted it is often advisable to work with locals. With regard to consumer propositions, every country in the world is different, and often there are also significant differences within countries. In the UK, for example, it can be more expensive to find a high-quality retail location outside London than inside London (even though the inexperienced might believe the contrary to be true as property is generally more expensive in London). This is because in cities outside London prime locations are in shorter supply and are more aggressively sought. Business-to-business practice also differs from country to country. Local businesses are often more inclined to trust and therefore do business with local businesses, but this is not always the case. It takes local knowledge to understand that some businesses in South-East Asia would rather take consulting advice from British or American firms than from local firms, not because of perceptions of superior capability but because of fears about confidentiality.

Franchising

Franchising and licensing are often considered by organisations that grow by replicating what they do overseas. Under a franchise arrangement a business develops a business system which in effect it sells to others, who then run their own small businesses using a tried and tested model. The fast-food industry has many franchise businesses, McDonald's perhaps being the best-known example. Under most franchise arrangements, the franchisee pays for the right to use the name, logo and merchandising, as well as essential elements of the business process. The franchisor provides training in the use of the business methodology and support. The arrangement is governed by a franchise agreement between the franchisor and its franchisees.

Franchising is one way in which businesses have sought scale without sacrificing the owner-managed qualities often associated with smaller businesses. For many would-be owner-managers, a franchise arrangement is one way of founding a business in which many of the usual risks of entrepreneurship are significantly reduced. For the franchisor, it allows rapid growth and access to capital. In terms of growth, the model enables franchisors to have their cake and eat it; business units stay relatively small, but the business as a whole can grow rapidly. Franchisees, however, are aware of the barriers to growth: the growth of each outlet will be constrained by its location. A franchisor that wishes to grow will need to acquire more franchises, perhaps becoming a master-franchise within a wider franchise network.

Not every business that has tried to franchise has been satisfied with the results. A business that chooses to franchise itself and replaces subsidiary businesses, directly run outlets and so forth with franchise income has to work harder at controlling important elements of the brand proposition such as quality and culture. In effect, direct supervision has to be replaced by careful selection of franchisees and by the controls set out in a carefully worded franchise agreement. Pret a Manger tried franchising in its early years, but the experiment petered out after a few stores. Starbucks has an ambivalent relationship with the concept. In some parts of the world, such as the Middle East, it is run in effect as one franchise, though even here it should be noted that stores tend to be owned by the regional partner rather than franchised. In the United States, where the business started, most Starbucks outlets are owned and operated by the company. Howard Schultz was interviewed shortly after his return to Starbucks as CEO in 2009 when growth was faltering. His comments, quoted in *Harvard Business Review* in July 2010, highlight the problems facing many successful CEOs when considering franchising:

> *You have to have 100% belief in your core reason for being. There was tremendous pressure in the first three of months after my return to dramatically change the strategy and the business model of the company. The marketplace was saying, "Starbucks needs to undo all these company-owned stores and franchise the system." That would have given us a war chest of cash and significantly increased return on capital. It is a good argument economically. It is a good argument for shareholder value. But it would have fractured the culture of the company. You cannot get out of this by trying to navigate with a different road map, one that is not true to yourself. You have to be authentic, you have to be true, and you have to believe in your heart that this is going to work.*

There are, however, many businesses that have made franchising work well. McDonald's has already been mentioned. Body Shop's early growth was through franchising, and it succeeded through not just the originality and appeal of the concept but also the robustness of the franchise arrangement and its ability to recruit franchise owners who shared the enthusiasms and vision of the founder.

Timing is important when franchising. A franchisor can attract franchisees only if the proposition it wants to franchise has a successful track record, which will take time to establish. Potential franchisees who are wooed too early might take the view that insufficient risks are mitigated and they might as well take all the risks themselves and set up on their own from first principles. Conversely, a franchisee who joins a franchise at the beginning might be able to negotiate to keep more of the value than one hoping to join a well-established franchise. Owners who have set up a successful business but are still wrestling with the fire-fighting that growth brings might be susceptible to an approach from a potential franchisee offering to open up a new territory, thus providing a route to expansion beyond their current management capacity and capability. As well as worrying about expanding their own business, successful business founders need to think about copycats. A franchise arrangement might provide a satisfactory compromise for a business looking to replicate.

Licensing

Licensing is a smaller-scale arrangement than franchising. A franchise governs many aspects of the business: brand, product, uniform, pricing, and so on. A licence usually gives the right to provide one or other of these elements. It therefore typically gives its user the legal right to use something that might otherwise be protected by, for example, a patent or trademark. It is another vehicle for facilitating the replication of a business.

9   The changing nature of growth

IN THE 19TH and much of the 20th century, businesses got bigger and bigger. The 21st century started with globalisation increasingly taken for granted as inevitable, with implications for the optimum size of the world's most powerful and influential businesses. In their book *The Alchemy of Growth*, Merhdad Baghai, Steve Coley and David White wrote:[23]

> *Growth is a noble pursuit. It creates new jobs for the community and wealth for shareholders. It can turn ordinary companies into stimulating environments where employees find a sense of purpose in their work ... Growth's transformative power is akin to the alchemy of old.*

However, in the wake of the financial crisis that started in 2008, public opinion has hardened against the influence exercised by some of the biggest organisations merely because of their size. Even the desirability of globalisation has been questioned. But size is not just a question of fashion or sentiment. As discussed in Chapter 4, the optimum size of businesses in some industries will always be smaller than in others. And some more general trends – particularly technological – have influenced the optimum size of organisations and therefore affected growth. This chapter discusses some of these general influences on organisational size and on growth and considers their implications.

Bigger is better

Other things being equal, bigger companies generally have the following advantages over smaller ones.

Economies of scale

The bigger an organisation the more it is able to make efficient use of its assets and resources. It can make better use of fixed-cost inputs; sales and output are likely to be more evenly distributed over time; and the use of internal resources can be planned more efficiently. It can achieve greater economies by buying materials and services in bulk. It is also more likely to be able to afford internal professional expertise: an HR department to deal with the increasing mountain of employment legislation; a marketing department to establish brand propositions; an IT department to build and maintain tailor-made systems infrastructures. Economies of scale are not endless, however. An organisation will reach a size where the management costs of holding it together outweigh the cost savings derived from scale; this is the point when diminishing returns to scale will set in.

Ronald Coase, a Nobel prize-winning economist, expounded his theory about the role and size of the organisation as a function of the optimum trade-off between costs and benefits in an article, "The Nature of the Firm", published in 1937. He compares what he calls transaction costs (the costs of doing a transaction in the open market) with organisation costs (the costs of an organisation performing the same task itself). The fact that organisation costs tend to be lower than the equivalent transaction costs helps explain why business organisations come into existence in the first place. But Coase's thinking has been extended to help determine the optimum size of an organisation. Using the transactional cost theory, a business will tend to be larger if:

- the costs of managing the business are lower and rise more slowly with the size of the business;
- the entrepreneur is less likely to make mistakes and the increase in mistakes decreases in proportion to the increase in size of the business;
- there are economies of scale with regard to costs of supplies and resources.

The first two costs will increase with the geographical distribution of the business's products and services and the increase in the range of products and services provided. Coase's theory helps explain why companies tend either to be in different geographic locations or to focus on particular types of business. It has also helped explain why some businesses have managed to grow so large: in effect their organisational costs are lower than their transactional costs, despite their exceptional size (examples are Standard Oil, General Motors and General Electric).

Market power

A bigger organisation will have a bigger market share, so it is more likely to be able to dictate terms to the market, particularly on prices. Smaller businesses have to accept the prices set by bigger organisations unless they can undercut them, which for many is unlikely as they will not be able to take advantage of economies of scale in the cost structure.

Credibility

A big organisation is often more credible than a smaller competitor. For example, small companies have long complained that the odds are stacked against them when they apply for government contracts. The huge amount of paperwork involved favours big organisations with the administrative resources to deal with it – but this is another economy of scale. Just as important is the IBM syndrome – that is, "no one ever got fired for buying from IBM" – even though the products of smaller, newer companies might be demonstrably superior or better suited to the customer's purpose. Buying from a big, well-established company is not as risky for a manager as buying from a less well-known company.

Credibility affects small companies in other ways, in particular their ability to receive favourable credit terms, to attract capable, ambitious staff, and to secure leases on premises.

Technology and the size of the firm

It could be argued that an implication of Coase's theory of the firm is that organisations such as General Motors or General Electric grew so big because they were more efficient at managing and implementing transactions internally than through the external market. Some have argued that modern developments in information technology, the internet in particular, have changed this. In their book, *Unleashing the Killer App*,[24] Larry Downes and Chunka Mui argue that the internet has dramatically reduced many transaction costs, particular those associated with the flow of information and payment. Big businesses have less of a comparative advantage than has been the case historically and small firms less of a disadvantage. Indeed, Downes and Mui predict a shift of influence from the large firms that have dominated the commercial landscape in the past two centuries to smaller firms. The "law of diminishing firms" has usurped the influential role previously occupied by the law of diminishing returns.

Not everyone agrees with Downes and Mui's thesis. Some, arguing from a theoretical standpoint, have noted that the internet has the effect of reducing organisational costs as well as transactional costs (as defined by Coase), and that organisational size is not necessarily affected. In practice, there is no doubt that in some ways modern technology does improve the position of small firms. Using the criteria outlined above, a small firm can use the internet to win positions of influence in the market quickly in ways not previously possible. It can be difficult to appreciate the true scale of an organisation behind a good website; problems of credibility that smaller firms have historically struggled with are thus mitigated.

At the same time, a networked world enhances the prospects of much more flexible organisational entities and eases the relationships between them. Internet technologies and structures have conspired to make previously omnipotent, giant companies seem weak and inflexible, and exposed them to attacks from organisations of a size that would previously have posed no threat. Regulators continue to struggle to keep pace with change in the music and publishing industries, for example.

However, although technology has empowered smaller organisations, the spectacular history of the growth of organisations such as Microsoft, Apple, Google and Facebook shows that technology can provide an environment in which organisations can grow very large. Perhaps it is the pace of change that technology has influenced even more than the optimum size of organisations. Facebook was founded only in 2004; by early 2011 it had over 600m users around the world and was reputedly worth more than $2 billion. The converse is also true – in some instances technology will exacerbate the speed of an organisation's decline. The well-publicised struggle of *Encyclopaedia Britannica* when confronted with the rise of the internet is just one example of a business model whose very existence has been threatened by technology, not helped by it. There will certainly be many more.

Small is beautiful

Technological change is just one force that continues to provoke questions about the optimal size for organisations. There have been others and there will be more.

British economist E.F. Schumacher's book, *Small is Beautiful: a study of economics as if people mattered*, was published in 1973 when the world was reeling from an oil crisis. It has been in print ever since, a testament to the fact that its thesis has found supporters in different economic circumstances and responding to different economic crises. Schumacher argues that focusing on output and technology is dehumanising, and that greater priority should be given to the meaning and dignity of economic activity and its use (or abuse) of natural resources than to efficiency and the thirst for profit. His conclusions cannot be reduced to a simplistic notion that small is good and big is bad; more characteristic of his thinking is the notion of "smallness within bigness", which takes him towards organisations that have worked hard to preserve the culture of the small as they grow bigger, looking to decentralisation and different types of organisational structure for help. Schumacher was also one of the earliest thinkers to express concerns about the relevance of GNP when assessing economic success, arguing that a better objective was to "obtain the maximum amount of well-being with the minimum amount of consumption". In some ways, therefore, Schumacher also heralds the "gross national happiness" movement (see Chapter 5).

Schumacher developed his thesis during the oil crises of the early 1970s. But economic crises have a habit of fostering supporters of small businesses. Conversely, big businesses are often held accountable for the crisis. Big banks, big car corporations and other big companies have been considered too big to fail as a consequence of the credit crunch of 2008, while smaller companies have gone to the wall. As economists and regulators try to find a way of ensuring that an economic crisis never happens again, big businesses and the practices and cultures they stand for are once more in the firing line. New visions are being developed for the next generation of managers – with implications for managers and their growth plans. In February 2009 Gary Hamel, a management guru, proposed in an article, "Moon shots for management", published in *Harvard Business Review*, a new programme of enquiry for business thinkers and a new set of challenges for managers. Many of his challenges touch on themes that Schumacher would have championed: "Eliminate the pathologies of formal hierarchy", "Reduce fear and increase trust", "Redefine the work of leadership", "Develop holistic performance measures". Others take careful aim at some of the traditional growth levers and measures:

> *Ensure that the work of management serves a higher purpose. Most companies strive to maximise shareholder wealth – a goal that is inadequate in many respects. As an emotional catalyst, wealth maximisation lacks the power to fully mobilise human energies. It is an insufficient defence when people question the legitimacy of corporate power. And it is not specific or compelling enough to spur renewal. For these reasons, tomorrow's management practices must focus on the achievement of socially significant and noble goals.*

Hamel's propositions, like Schumacher's, are not entirely new. Adam Smith's first book was not *The Wealth of Nations*, often cited as the bible of free-market economics, but *The Theory of Moral Sentiments*, in which he argues that while "prudence" is "of all virtues that which is most helpful to the individual", it is "humanity, justice, generosity, and public spirit" that are "the qualities most useful to others".[25] Smith does not mention the "noble pursuit" of growth, at least not in this context. Hamel's exhortation that we should reconsider our commercial and economic priorities suggests that debates about the role and value of growth will have a long future as well as a long history.

Glossary: an A–Z of growth

Accounts

In their published form and in the United States these are often called financial statements, but the two terms are used interchangeably.

The problem with accounts is that they look backwards and businesses with ambition to grow are interested in looking forwards. Audited accounts are even more problematic in that they look backwards from a point that is itself likely to be several months old.

It takes years to qualify as an accountant but not so long to be able to get a good enough grip on accounting principles for commercial purposes. Here are a few tips for the general user of accounts in growing businesses:

- Accounting is an art not a science.
- With regard to published financial statements, different countries and jurisdictions have developed over the years different sets of accounting standards. Financial statements of different companies within the same country are therefore easier to compare than the financial statements of companies from different countries. The development of International Financial Reporting Standards has made some progress towards international standardisation, but it is still only a start.
- There are always two stories: the story that the directors are trying to tell and the story that they are trying to hide.
- The devil is in the detail. The notes at the back of sets of accounts often provide the only clues as to what is hidden in the more frequently read pages at the front.

- **Cash flow** is as important if not more so than profit in a growing business, so check the funds statements, or statement of cash flows, as well as the income statements and **balance sheets**.

- In a relatively young business, management accounts (or whatever passes for internal management information) are often a more useful source of information for an outsider than the published financial statements. These are the documents that the managers use to take decisions, and they are likely to be more up to date.

Accounts payable
See **creditors**.

Accounts receivable
See **debtors**.

Accruals accounting and cash accounting
Under the accruals concept, accounting revenue and costs are recognised as they are earned or incurred and not as the money is received or paid. Under cash accounting the reverse is true. Standard accounting practice follows the accruals rather than the cash approach, as this ensures that actual business performance is reported rather than just cash movements. But it is the cause of much confusion in the minds of those not used to reading **accounts**. It is possible for a business to show a profit but go bust for lack of cash. The distinction is of particular importance to smaller growing businesses where cash is always under pressure.

Acquisitions
See **mergers and acquisitions**.

Additional paid-in capital
See **share capital and share premium account**.

Alternative Investment Market

London's junior stockmarket. Rather than list on the main market, companies might choose to list on the Alternative Investment Market (AIM). It costs less and there are fewer rules, and it is aimed at smaller, younger companies that are perhaps not ready for the full market. But it is also less prestigious, is less liquid and provides less access to funds. There are no real equivalents to the AIM in the United States, which is why approximately 70 American companies were listed on it in early 2011. Not right for venture capital and too small for NASDAQ, these companies found the AIM the most appropriate source of finance.

There have been attempts to set up junior markets elsewhere in the world, including Alternext (part of Euronext in Paris and Amsterdam), Catalyst in Singapore and the Growth Enterprise Market (GEM) in Hong Kong. However, none of these has so far replicated the AIM's success.
See Chapter 6.

Amortisation

See **depreciation**.

Ansoff matrix

Commonly used when analysing growth options, particularly new products and markets. This two-by-two matrix (see Figure 3.3 on page 49) is designed to reduce to manageable proportions the numerous strategic alternatives open to a business. The model provides a useful way of evaluating the risk inherent in a new initiative. Selling a new product to a new market is much more risky than selling a new product to an existing market or an existing product to a new market. Though many would argue that doing nothing is probably the riskiest of all.
See Chapter 3.

Arm's length

An arm's length transaction is conducted according to normal business rules as if it was between third parties. The term is often used for deals between two parties who have a relationship with each other to indicate that the relationship has not prejudiced the deal. **Entrepreneurs** notoriously have difficulty with the concept.

Articles of association

Articles of incorporation in the United States. In effect the constitution of the company governing internal affairs such as share issues, directors' elections, **dividend** policies. Most business owners pay too little attention to the articles when the business is founded; many subsequently regret such casualness, particularly if members of the founding team fall out and start fighting for control. Well-advised business owners with growth ambitions read the small print carefully and work out the implications for the business under different scenarios. In the UK, before the Companies Act 2006, the **memorandum of association** was also important, but most of the constitutional provisions that used to matter are now incorporated within the articles.

Articles of incorporation

See **articles of association.**

Asset-based finance

See **factoring.**

Asset turnover

A commonly used ratio in financial analysis is turnover/total assets. It indicates how efficient a company is at using the resources tied up in the business to generate activity. In practice, many figures on the **balance sheet** (notably the long-term assets and liabilities) are notoriously unreliable, particularly as measures of the amount of resources tied up, when used for analysis and decision-making. This is because the numbers cited are influenced far more by accounting policy and convention than by any realisable notion of market worth.

Audit report

A report by independent auditors, indicating their opinion as to whether the financial statements are free from material error. A "clean" report is what most companies aim for. A "qualified" report states why a clean report cannot be given. Many smaller companies in the UK and the EU are exempt from what is otherwise a statutory requirement to have an audit. The only American incorporated companies required to have an audit are publicly traded ones or where it is specified in a debt or equity agreement (as in the UK and the EU, where a bank loan agreement may require an audit regardless of the size of the company). There are no size-related audit exemptions in the United States.

Bad debt

Not all **debtors** pay what they owe. Such debts are either doubtful or bad. A bad debt is removed from the **balance sheet** and written off to the income statement (profit and loss account). Debt management is a critical part of cash management. Many growing businesses do not give it the attention it deserves.

Balance sheet

A statement at a specific date of the assets and liabilities of a business, prepared using certain assumptions. It shows where the money came from originally and in which parts of the business it is invested at the balance-sheet date. It is a poor indicator of the value of a business, particularly a rapidly growing one, because of the conventions used in its construction.

Benchmarking

Businesses often like to compare themselves with other businesses. When formalised the process is called benchmarking. Some consultants have earned good money selling benchmarking services. Critics argue that it fosters a me-too mentality. However, many growing businesses do not know much about their competitors or their offerings. Benchmarking can equally well be used as a basis for a differentiation strategy as for a me-too strategy. Companies can usefully benchmark all sorts of things. In many instances certification programmes help to provide benchmarking standards, such as the ISO90001 quality standard which is increasingly recognised around the world. Many companies attempt to benchmark salary levels against important competitors.

Board of directors

The group of individuals with statutory responsibility for running the business of an incorporated company. Directors are appointed by **shareholders**. If you have a majority of the shares you can control the composition of the board, but you cannot control the management of the business unless you sit on the board. The majority of board members in big businesses are now commonly **non-executive** or outside directors so the day-to-day task of running the business is delegated to an executive or **management team**.

Book value

The amount at which an item (usually an asset) is recorded in the books. Value often has little to do with the amount recorded. Usually items are recorded at the lower of cost or net realisable value. In the UK, however, there are also provisions in accounting practice for revaluing some types of asset. Consequently, in any set of **accounts** some items might appear at cost, some at what a business expects to get for them if sold, and some at what an independent valuer thinks they might be worth. In the United States, the Financial Standards Accounting Board does not allow the upward revaluation of fixed assets.

Boston matrix

Another of those two-by-two boxes on which business analysis seems so dependent (see Figure 3.1 on page 45). This one was invented by the Boston Consulting Group. At its simplest the matrix helps identify future product development options and rationalise expectations. It usefully illustrates how it is that the most exciting areas of the business often make little money, and why it is that the most cash-generative areas of the business are seen as boring. If initiatives are unlikely to become cash cows in the future, they are not worth focusing on. If they are likely to become cash cows, it may be worth taking a loss on them now.

See Chapter 3.

Break-even analysis

Determines how big a business needs to be to generate a profit. It is based on the assumption that some costs are fixed and some are variable; if the business grows, it will earn enough to cover the fixed costs and will become cash-positive. Break-even analysis is also used when assessing individual projects.
See Chapter 5.

Business angel

A name given to a wealthy individual interested in investing in private businesses – often one of the few sources of funds for companies in the notorious funding gap – when they are too big to rely on the founders' pockets, not big enough to interest the institutional sources of equity financing (such as **venture capital** or **private equity**) and insufficiently creditworthy to be able to raise debt from banks. Business angels come in all shapes and sizes, with different specialisms, preferences and expectations.
See Chapter 5.

Business plan

Some businesses think they need to prepare a business plan only because a bank will demand one before considering a loan. Some also argue that time spent planning is futile as what is planned and what happens bear little relation to each other. Time spent planning, however, usually pays rewards – even if reality turns out differently – if only because it makes businesses think about the future. Indeed, the act of planning is more valuable than the plan that results. Nonetheless, the document provides a business with something to monitor progress against.
See Chapter 4.

Capital

A word with many meanings. Some of the most common are as follows:

- At the bottom of the **balance sheet** it refers to the **shareholders'** financial interest in the business.
- It is used more loosely to describe all long-term financial stakes in the business, including loans (long-term **creditors**).
- When associated with expenditure, it refers to the purchase of **fixed assets** or long-term investment.

Capital expenditure

Expenditure on an item the benefits of which it is hoped will be derived over a long period – certainly one stretching over several years of financial statements. Rather than being written off against profit in the year of acquisition, a capital item will be depreciated or amortised over its useful life. (See **depreciation** and **revenue expenditure**.)

Capital surplus

American term for share premium account. (See **share capital and share premium account**.)

Cash

For accountants, not just coins and notes in the cash box, but bank balances and other investments that are exceptionally secure and readily converted into cash. Nothing is more important to a business than cash, and few things are less well understood. Cash management is about understanding the nature of the cash cycle: how long it takes to convert cash tied up on the **balance sheet** in stock and debt into cash in the bank, and the extent to which the drain represented by that cash cycle widens as the order book grows and the business expands. It is possible for a profitable company to go bust because it grows faster than can be sustained by the cash-generative capabilities of the business. That gap must be plugged somehow, either with external finance or by changing the dynamics of the cash cycle itself. See Chapter 6.

Cash flow, cash flow forecast

Money coming in (or going out) in the form of cash. If the net flow is inwards, cash flow is called positive; if the net flow is outwards, it is called negative. A cash flow forecast gives the expected dates of cash flows in and out of the business. Cash flow is an important concept in **discounted cash flow** calculations. It is also important in staying alive – cash is the blood of a business.
See Chapter 5.

Cash flow statement

This indicates the cash generated by the business (as opposed to the profit). It helps readers assess the **liquidity** of a business.

Change

A manager of a business ambitious for growth who is not involved in change will not be a manager for long. Change and growth are inextricably linked. A big business is not a larger version of a smaller one. A business has to evolve as well as grow if its growth is to be sustainable. In other words, a business has to grow up as well as grow.
See Chapters 2 and 4.

Common stock

American term for ordinary shares (see **share capital** and **shareholders**).

Consolidated statement

Companies are often interconnected under the same ownership. Consolidated statements are statements or **accounts** that give figures for the various parts of a group added together. It is often difficult to get accounts or statements for the individual businesses themselves.

Control

A crucial decision for an **entrepreneur** is when, or if, to give up control of a business. Issues related to this include confusion over control and ownership. You do not have to own all of the company to control it. Many entrepreneurs are reluctant to allow others to have a slice of the equity, and this can constrain the growth of the business. It is possible to allow others in on the action without giving up control. For example, all other things being equal, shareholders, though they might otherwise have to concede some rights to minority shareholders, give up control over a company only if they lose control over the majority of the shares. However, majority shareholders need to be careful when they take in financial investors. In some cases, clauses in the documentation governing an investment in the business by an institutional equity investor (such as a venture capitalist) compromise the control of the majority shareholder.

Convertible

A convertible bond or loan stock is debt that has the potential to be converted into equity in the future if certain conditions are fulfilled. A convertible preferred or preference share is one that has the potential for conversion into an ordinary share. Convertible debt is often used by venture capitalists as part of a funding package. If business targets are not met, the debt is converted to equity, often reallocating control of the business from the owner to the financier in the process.
See Chapter 5.

Core competence

A term often used by those interested in corporate strategy. Early strategists were mostly concerned with analysing the market and the competition. Core competence advocates, including Gary Hamel and C.K. Pralahad, authors of *Competing for the Future*, argue that businesses should first look inwards at what they are best at and what makes them different.[26] Businesses that understand their own core competences are rare. Typically, younger businesses trust gut feelings rather than analysis. They are good at making assertions about the nature of their products, services and competition, but have little evidence to back them up. Identifying core competences is the first step towards developing critical success factors, which can be measured by **key performance indicators**.
See Chapters 3 and 6.

Corporate bond

A form of long-term debt finance whereby a company quotes its long-term debt on the stockmarket.
See Chapter 6.

Cost of capital

The amount that needs to be paid to **shareholders** and long-term lenders to keep them happy. This is a simple definition of a complex concept. In essence, cost of capital has two main components: cost of equity (what needs to be paid to shareholders) and cost of debt (the interest that is paid to long-term **debt holders** or **debenture** holders, who are among a company's **creditors**).

Creditors

Those to whom a business owes money, usually split between short-term creditors (sometimes called **current liabilities**) and long-term creditors. In the United States, trade creditors are called accounts payable. Creditors could include amounts owed to banks, suppliers, tax authorities, and so on. Managing short-term creditors, particularly trade creditors, is another important part of **cash** management in a growing business.
See Chapter 5.

Culture

All those undocumented and informal things that distinguish one business from another, often best understood by identifying what is "not done" or "not talked about" – things that are so obvious that no one questions them. Culture is difficult to change (not least because it is so difficult to talk about). But a failure to adapt or change the organisational culture is often the reason change initiatives fail to change anything. Small organisations arguably do not have cultures; they have personalities, reflecting usually that of the founder. As the business grows, the founder's personality has less influence – a matter of simple mathematics, of course. In many ways, defining and influencing organisational culture are simply an attempt to make up for the waning influence of the founder. Awareness of a business's culture and its implications gives management an important additional set of levers and controls. See Chapter 7.

Cumulative

Often used as part of a long label to describe a funding mechanism, such as cumulative, convertible participating preferred share (or stock). In this sense, cumulative usually refers to the **dividend** on the share, which is probably fixed on a preferred share. If it is not paid in a year, the right to the dividend is not lost, it is rolled forward.

Current assets

A component of **working capital** comprising stock, cash and **debtors**; the short-term assets of a business that are held as cash or that may be converted into cash within one year.

Current liabilities

Commonly used to describe those **creditors** that are payable in the short term – that is, payable within one year.

Current ratio

A ratio used in analysing the financial statements, usually defined as current assets/current liabilities. This gives an indication of **liquidity,** that is, the extent to which the business is able to pay its short-term **creditors** with cash and assets easily convertible to cash. It is an important ratio for any business in which cash is an issue, as it often is for growing businesses. Ideally, the figure should be more than 1. In other words, the business is demonstrably able to meet its short-term liabilities with cash, quasi-cash or soon-to-be cash on the **balance sheet.** See **quick ratio.**

Debenture

A form of long-term **debt finance** (a **creditor**). In the UK, the term usually refers to debt secured on an asset of a business. In the United States, it usually refers to an unsecured **corporate bond.**
See Chapter 6.

Debt factoring

See **factoring**.

Debt finance

Also known as loan capital. Long-term loans offered to a business, sometimes in the form of a **debenture** or **corporate bond**.

Debt holder

A long-term debt holder (sometimes called a bond holder) is different from a **shareholder**. A debt holder is a **creditor** of the business not a **debtor**, and receives a fixed amount of interest at regular intervals. A shareholder owns the business, and may receive a **dividend** but has no guarantee. If the business goes bankrupt, a shareholder will rank behind a debt holder in terms of who gets paid. (See **equity finance**.) See Chapter 6.

Debtors

Those who owe money to a business. In the United States, trade debtors are called accounts receivable. A debtor is an asset of a business whereas a **creditor** is a liability. **Debt finance**, however, is all about a business owing money to someone else.

Depreciation

A way of allocating the cost of a tangible fixed asset to the income statement (profit and loss account) bit by bit over the life of the asset rather than writing it off in the period in which it is bought. It may also be considered a measure of wear and tear. **Intangible assets** do not depreciate, they amortise, but it is the same thing. They are both non-cash adjustments to the **accounts**, and are subject to the judgment exercised by accountants.

Discounted cash flow

A complicated mechanism frequently used as part of investment appraisal, or in deciding whether to pursue a long-term project. Essentially, discounted cash flow (DCF) attempts to measure and compare all the positive and negative **cash flows** projected to arise from a project, discounting by a predetermined amount cash flows that occur in the future using a figure known as the discount factor. The logic behind DCF is complicated, but is best summarised by accepting that $10 received today is worth more than a promise today of receiving $10 next year, so to make the comparison fair next year's $10 needs to be valued at less than $10 today. The size of the discount depends on how big the risk is that you will never see the money.

DCF is much used by financiers as part of their evaluation of investment opportunities. It is fraught with difficulty, however. First, the cash flows are future cash flows and are estimates. Second, slight changes in the discount factor can have enormous effects on the calculation. That some big corporations have worked out their discount factor to four decimal places suggests that determining discount factors is more important than it should be. Unfortunately for scientists, the biggest component of risk (and therefore determinant of the discount factor) is the unpredictability of future events.

Diversification

When a business seeks to involve itself in activities that are essentially different from its current activities. Some years ago a well-diversified 'conglomerate' was often thought of as a desirable business structure to aim for. Now that 'core-competence' has become fashionable, diversification as a business strategy has fallen out of favour. Managers are now encouraged to stick to their knitting. Diversifying is something that investors are encouraged to do instead – advice that investors in young businesses are particularly encouraged to heed.

Dividend

A formal payment made to a shareholder from time to time out of profits. The concept is simple. A business makes money (profit). Some of this is kept in the business for investment; some is needed to pay **creditors** and the tax authorities; the rest might be distributed to the owners of the business (the **shareholders**) in the form of a dividend. Dividends are not an expense, they are a mechanism for distributing profit – so it is rarely possible to distribute a dividend unless a business has distributable reserves (essentially retained profits) on the **balance sheet**.

Those involved in growing businesses often wear several hats. As owner-managers, for example, they can pay themselves as employees with wages and bonuses, and as owners with dividends. The tax implications of doing one rather than the other differ – and doing something for tax reasons often confuses other more important issues, such as understanding the difference between management and ownership. Either all the shareholders with shares of the same class get a dividend or none of them do. A company cannot pick and choose.

Due diligence

Investigations carried out by parties interested in doing a deal. A company seeking to acquire another might appoint a firm of accountants to do due diligence on the target, examining its financial statements, projections, and so on. An investor or a bank seeking to finance such an acquisition might perform its own due diligence (or appoint a firm of accountants to do it for them). Due diligence usually starts with the financial statements and the stories they are trying to tell, or not tell, but then wanders far wider into all aspects of commercial activity, the market, the strength of the **management team**, and so on.

Earnings per share

Often abbreviated to EPS, usually defined as the amount of profit after tax and interest that has been earned by each ordinary share.

Empowerment

Management speak for the useful concept of giving staff the authority and wherewithal to take decisions for themselves. Intelligently managed, empowerment can lead to better, quicker decisions and therefore help a business to grow. But the concept can be difficult to introduce, partly because some managers confuse empowerment with abdication or passing the blame, and many staff – when push comes to shove – quite like being told what to do.

See Chapters 2, 4 and 7.

Entrepreneur

In essence, the spark behind an organisation who gets it from the drawing-board into profit, in contrast to the inventor who merely gets the idea onto the drawing-board – though, of course, some inventors are also entrepreneurs. At the heart of the entrepreneurial urge is the desire to do your own thing, a yearning for independence, a determination that something can be done better by you than by someone else. In entrepreneurship, therefore, qualities of personality are perhaps more important than qualities of ability, or a yearning for riches.

Entrepreneurs are committed, enthusiastic, energetic motivators with a willingness to accept risk. Although motivated by the desire for independence, entrepreneurs are not necessarily loners (many are two or more person teams), nor are they reckless gamblers – the risk is usually calculated. But they are people who do not like being told no. They ask "why not?" rather than "why?" and a sophisticated view is that they are perhaps best at marshalling **intangible assets** to make up for an absence of tangible assets to achieve a particular goal. At the heart of entrepreneurship therefore is a paradox. On the one hand it is all about making concrete the abstract. On the other hand it is all about not losing heart when the only thing you have on your side is the abstract. (See **team**.)

See Chapters 6 and 7.

Equity finance

Finance for a business provided by ordinary **shareholders** in return for ownership of the business. (See **debt finance**.)

See Chapter 6.

Factoring

Once thought of as the corporate equivalent of a visit to the pawnbroker, debt factoring and other forms of asset-based finance are increasingly seen as important additions to the financial armoury of growing businesses. And, bearing in mind that small businesses in particular have few sources of finance on which to draw, a change of attitude towards factoring can only be a good thing. Factoring or invoice discounting comes in several forms. The basic principle

involves raising money from a bank or specialist finance house either by selling your trade **debtors** (factoring) or by using trade debtors as security for a loan (invoice discounting). Critics argue that asset-based finance is expensive. But enthusiasts note that most small businesses fund themselves with nothing cheaper than an overdraft, which can have hidden costs given that it is repayable on demand and banks usually want their money back when it is most needed. Another advantage is that a business's capacity for raising asset-based finance increases as it grows.
See Chapter 6.

Family business

The majority of businesses worldwide are family businesses, but only a small proportion of these survive to the third generation, suggesting that family and business are not natural bedfellows. This has important implications for businesses with ambitions to grow. Successful family businesses spend a lot of time and money establishing mechanisms to ensure the successful survival of the business as one generation hands over the reins to another, designed to ensure the interests of business and family are met.
See Chapter 4.

Fixed assets

Assets that have been acquired not for resale but for use by the business in the longer term. They may be tangible (physical objects) or intangible (such as goodwill or patents).

Flotation

See **initial public offering**.

Games

Much recent thinking on business strategy has sought inspiration in other disciplines. Modern maths has proved fertile territory – with chaos theory and game theory providing lateral lines of thought – particularly for those interested in the subtleties of relationships between competitors and customers and suppliers. Try thinking of competitors

as fellow players in a game for a change rather than enemies from some evil empire. To what extent are all players in a market useful to each other? Adam Brandenburger and Barry Nalebuff, in their book *Co-Opetition*, invent and consider new roles in the game of business.[27] For example, there are "complementors", whose activity in the market adds value to your own. Video film is a well-known example, first seen by the cinema industry as a threat and then welcomed for the additional revenue it provided once the period of a film's general release had effectively ended. The evolution of the DVD and the increasing popularity of downloadable films are reminders that markets never stay still. Businesses that are keen to grow need to understand the subtleties of their markets, and this type of thinking adds some useful insight.
See Chapter 3.

Gearing

Commonly used in the UK to refer to the level of long-term debt in a business (that is, the proportion of long-term **creditors** to **shareholders' funds** or owners' equity). In the United States the term is leverage. A highly geared or leveraged company is one whose **balance sheet** shows a large amount owing to long-term creditors proportional to shareholder funding. Such companies are often thought to be financially risky as debt carries an interest charge that must be paid whether business is good or bad. A lowly geared company, however, with a high proportion of shareholder or **equity finance**, can always not pay a **dividend**. However, in the longer term **debt finance** is usually thought of as less expensive than equity finance, not just because it is less risky but also because interest is tax deductible.
See Chapter 6.

Gross profit

The amount of profit derived from a business's operations, ignoring overheads and other fixed costs (see **net profit**). For retailing businesses, therefore, gross profit is simply sales less the cost of goods sold. In businesses such as professional services, gross profit is a less meaningful concept.
See Chapter 5.

Gross profit margin

Gross profit as a percentage of revenue or **turnover**.
See Chapter 5.

Incentives

Staff incentives take many forms. Cash bonuses are the simplest way of encouraging short-term performance, but those who implement bonus schemes are often surprised by how little impact they seem to have on the conduct of some employees. Management performance is often rewarded with forms of equity or quasi-equity. But as well as being much more expensive to implement, such mechanisms run the risk of confusing management with ownership – a rock and a hard place with which **family businesses** in particular are only too familiar.
See Chapter 7.

Income

See **turnover**.

Incorporation

The act of turning an organisation into a limited company (or limited liability **partnership**), thus offering those who invest their money (**shareholders** in the case of a company) the benefit of limited liability with respect to the company's **creditors**. If a company goes bust, the shareholders lose only the money they invested and possibly some pride. If an unincorporated business goes bust, the business's owners are personally liable for any debts. With the protection of limited liability comes the requirement to publish **accounts** and in many circumstances to have them audited, though smaller businesses, and in some jurisdictions all private businesses, are often exempt from the full force of the regulations. Furthermore, the protection from creditors offered to directors by incorporation does not apply if they have given personal guarantees or, depending on the circumstances, if they allow the business to trade while insolvent.

Initial public offering

When a company's shares are offered for sale to the public for the first time, often abbreviated to IPO. The process is also known as flotation. See Chapter 6.

Insolvency

Not necessarily the end of the road. A term loosely applied to several states of precarious existence either side of the terminal line, from some of which – receivership, administration, Chapter 11, and so on – there is often a route back.

Intangible assets

Long-term assets of a business that have no physical existence, such as goodwill, patents, brands.

Interest

There are several meanings. The commonest are as follows:

- The amount charged by and paid to **creditors**.
- A financial investment in something.
- A non-financial involvement in something.

Interest cover

The ability of a business to pay its long-term **creditors** the interest they demand. Often expressed as a ratio (profit before interest and tax/interest) used in determining a business's **liquidity**.

Internal rate of return

A term associated with **discounted cash flow**. The internal rate of return (IRR) is the discount factor at which all the present and future positive and negative **cash flows** associated with a project added together total zero. Businesses often have target IRR figures below which they reject any proposed investment or **capital expenditure**. Institutional investors have a target IRR from their investments.

Intrapreneur

A senior manager given the task of setting up a new business within the context of a large organisation. Intrapreneurship has some of the characteristics of **entrepreneurship**, but in its access to corporate resources and its accountability to corporate management it is quite different.

Inventory

American term for **stock**.

Invoice discounting

See **factoring**.

Key performance indicator

The measure that matters most in a business. Key performance indicators (KPIs) are closely connected to a business's strategy, and the board should pay attention to them.

The KISS principle

Short for keep it simple stupid, a fundamental principle for much management. It is often ignored when growing a business when the temptation to complicate unnecessarily can be significant. Einstein refined the principle: "Keep things as simple as possible – but no simpler."
See Chapter 7.

Leader

Much has been written about leadership and the distinction between leadership and management. Both are critical to a successful organisation, but if management is mostly about effectively delivering the present, leadership is increasingly identified with **change**. Leadership, of course, can be collective, although in Anglo-American business culture the cult of the business leader as individual hero (and villain) is strong.

Successful start-ups are often rich in leadership but poor in management, which does not matter until they reach a size when the "suits" need to be brought in to ensure the bundle of resources that is the business does what it has to do effectively and efficiently. Conversely, there are many established businesses that are rich in management and poor in leadership as a consequence of having let the "suits" take over and squeeze the life, personality and spirit out of the business.

See Chapters 2 and 7.

Learning organisation

A fashionable management buzzword in the early 1990s. A learning organisation is an organisation that learns as an organisation through a co-ordinated approach to the learning of its individual members. Growing businesses need to change as they grow. Therefore they need to be learning organisations.

Leverage

See **gearing**.

Limited liability company

See **incorporation**.

Limited liability partnership

See **partnership**.

Liquidation

The end of the road for a business: what remains is broken up, converted to cash and distributed first to the **creditors** then, if there is anything left, to the **shareholders**. (See **insolvency**.)

Liquidity

How easily a business's assets may be converted into cash.

Listed company

A company whose shares are publicly quoted on a stockmarket. See Chapter 6.

Loan capital

See **debt finance**.

Losses

Bad news if maintained in the long term, of course, but for tax purposes losses can often be offset against profits in another period or part of the business.

Management buy-in

Or MBI. When outsiders buy a business and put themselves or another **management team** in as management.

Management buy-out

When the managers of a business buy it from the owners. The managers are often seen as sensible people to sell the business to: they know the business well, and they may believe that without the current owners breathing down their necks they can do a better job. Good business opportunities do not come cheap, however, and management buy-outs (MBOs) are often encumbered with a lot of external finance provided by, say, venture capitalists, who insist on having a **non-executive director** on the board as well as an ownership share of the business. Besides, managers with their eyes on an MBO are managers with an inherent conflict of interest. If they run the business badly they might be able to buy it cheaply, and they certainly might be distracted from the day-to-day task of management. Because of this, many large companies have a policy of not countenancing any MBOs, so managers know it is not worth worrying about it.

Management team

The group responsible for managing the business; not necessarily the same as the **board of directors**.
See Chapter 7.

Market capitalisation

The market value of each share in a **listed company** multiplied by the number of shares issued. This gives a measure of what the business is worth. Market capitalisation has nothing to do with any figure quoted on the face of the **balance sheet**, which is prepared under historical cost conventions and reflects the amount of money originally paid for shares when they were issued, not the price at which they change hands today.

Memorandum of association

In the UK, a document that used to be an important constitutional statement of a company's relationship with the outside world, including name, nationality, initial shareholders, and so on. Since revisions to the companies acts in the UK, the memorandum has much reduced significance and the sections that matter are now included in the **articles of association**.

Mergers and acquisitions

There are no such things as mergers, only takeovers, argue cynics. The sad thing about mergers and acquisitions is that, as research shows, the majority of them fail to deliver the planned and promised benefits. The good thing is that the chance of failure does not seem to stem the flood of **management teams** willing to give it a go.

Technically, a merger involves the creation of a new company from the union of two independent companies. It involves batteries of advisers: financiers to provide the wherewithal; lawyers to create the documentation; and accountants to conduct due diligence on each of the parties on the part of the various interested parties. And then there are the people issues: regulations to be complied with, and the concerns and worries of employees, customers and suppliers affected by the deal but not party to it.

An acquisition is when one business organisation buys another, or buys enough of the shares of another to gain control of it. The majority of acquisitions fail to meet their objectives. What makes sense on paper often makes less sense in reality. Consolidating financial statements is much easier than integrating a new business. It is common

for the acquiring company to focus on getting the numbers right and not put enough time or resources into sorting out the softer issues, such as **culture**, systems, processes, "the way things are done around here". It is what happens after the acquisition that will determine if it works, not what happens before. Some argue that business owners are usually advised to focus more on when to sell their business than when to buy someone else's. (See **control**.)
See Chapter 8.

Mezzanine finance
Finance provided "in the middle", between debt and equity, and sharing some of the characteristics of both. Often a feature of **venture capital** and **private equity** deals.
See Chapter 6.

MIFROG
The maximum internally financed rate of growth – a way of determining how quickly a business might grow without overtrading.
See Chapter 5.

Net current assets
Current assets – current liabilities.

Net present value
Or NPV, used in **discounted cash flow** calculations to describe the aggregate value of all the present and future **cash flows** arising from an investment after applying the discount factor to adjust future cash flows to be comparable with present cash flows.

Net profit
Gross profit minus expenses, overheads, and so on, but before **dividends** and tax.
See Chapter 5

Non-executive director

An executive director has a day-to-day management role in a business; a non-executive director does not. An executive director probably has an employment contract, and all the duties and worries of employment and management as well as those imposed by statute and by the company's articles on the director. Non-executive directors have to focus on the duties of a director. This can leave them with responsibilities and duties but no hands-on control or real-time access to information.

Non-executive directors can provide input to strategy. They can also help boards when conflicts of interest arise, such as directors' remuneration and dealing with auditors. Many boards have a non-executive chairman. In young businesses, non-executive directors can lend credibility to the **management team** (so important when seeking business or finance). They can also bring valuable experience of the problems likely at the next stages of company evolution, and help prepare the growing business for them.
See Chapter 7.

Notes to the accounts

An important part of sets of **accounts** or financial statements is the notes that follow them. They are a source of further information, and often where the important information is buried.

Operating cash cycle

All businesses in effect process cash. A manufacturer buys materials and labour that are paid for after an interval. The raw materials are used to make products that sit as stock until sold, with payment made after another period of time. The passage of cash from a business's customers to the business itself and from the business to its suppliers is the operating cash cycle. Understanding the components of the operating cash cycle, and how they relate to the long-term financing needs of the business, is a critical part of managing the business.
See Chapter 6.

Operating lease

A mechanism for acquiring the right to use an asset without the intention to purchase it outright or under hire purchase, and so on.

Operating profit

Profit derived from operations. Sometimes used synonymously with **net profit** (net income).

Ordinary share

The American term is common stock. See **shareholders**.

Overtrading

When a profitable business runs short of cash because it is growing too quickly and cannot finance its growth. Growing businesses need to finance their growth. The bigger they are the more cash they need to oil the wheels, and that cash has to come from somewhere. The most obvious sources are profits (internal finance), debt or more equity.
See Chapter 6.

Partnership

A form of unincorporated enterprise in which a group of individuals work together in a business and share the profits and **losses**. In most forms of partnership the partners do not have the benefit of limited liability, so they are personally liable for the debts of the business. So why would anyone bother? Sometimes there is no choice and individuals are obliged to form partnerships either by law or by industry regulation (for example, accounting and law). Others choose to remain partnerships and benefit from administrative economies (for example, they do not need an audit) and a degree of secrecy not permitted in limited companies (for example, partnerships do not have to publish **accounts**).

In recent years partnerships have been allowed to become limited liability partnerships (LLPs). This offers some of the tax advantages of being in a partnership and some limits to the liability of the partners for each other's actions, along with an obligation to publish accounts.

Many have been prepared to pay the price, and this form of incorporation has proved popular for start-ups.

Personal agenda

In addressing the personal issues at the heart of a growing business it is imperative to recognise any conflicting roles. Each role – whether director, shareholder, manager, employee, spouse, friend or parent – involves a set of tasks and objectives potentially conflict. **Entrepreneurs** need to know what hat to wear and when. When times get tough (which they will) they need to know which set of objectives takes priority or they will be in a weak position compared with other stakeholders, who either have a simpler set of objectives or have simply worked out where their priorities lie.

Preferred or preference shares

The American term is preferred or preference stock. See **shareholders**. See Chapter 6.

Price/earnings ratio

The market price of a share divided by the **earnings per share**. Applied backwards, the price/earnings (P/E) ratio is often used to value a business that is to be sold: it finds the P/E ratio of a similar business and applies it to its profits and sees what value is obtained. Although less scientific than other valuation techniques (such as **discounted cash flow**), the P/E ratio is simple to apply and is commonly used. Private companies take the P/E ratio of a listed company in the same industry and use it themselves, after applying a discount to account for the fact that privately held shares are less valuable than listed shares because they are less liquid.

Private equity

A term used for private equity investment in established businesses, and **venture capital** for private equity funding of young businesses. See Chapter 6.

Product life cycle

Organisations have life cycles (see growth models in Chapter 2) and industries have life cycles (see Chapter 3). Products do too.

Profit

Often called income in the United States. Profit is one of the most important, yet most misunderstood, concepts in business. At its simplest, it is what is left over from sales (revenue) after costs have been deducted:

- net profit is what is left over after all costs (except tax) have been deducted;
- gross profit is calculated by deducting only those costs directly related to the sale, that is, not deducting overheads or back-office costs.

  Other common labels include:

- net profit before tax (PBT);
- earnings before interest, tax, depreciation and amortisation (EBITDA).

See Chapter 5.

Quick ratio

Another popular measure of **liquidity**. It is similar to the **current ratio**, but ignores stock, thus giving a clearer picture of a business's ability to meet its **current liabilities**.
See Chapter 5.

Retained profits

An entry on the **balance sheet** indicating the **cumulative** profit retained in the business (that is, the aggregate of profits minus **dividends** paid each year).

Retirement

The least noticed of the big three "Rs": recruitment, redundancy and retirement. The concept of retirement is at last being rethought. In Europe it is often assumed that this is because of age discrimination legislation, but in reality it is because of fundamental economic and demographic changes that affect all Western economies, including the United States, which has not been subject to the same regulatory pressure. For many people retirement is not financially attractive; they are also living longer than earlier generations. Businesses with ambitions for growth are beginning to find roles for older employees, taking advantage of their experience and contacts. Employees beyond the traditional age of retirement know more and need less.

Return on capital employed (ROCE)

Or return on invested capital (ROIC). A commonly used ratio in financial analysis that gives some indication of the relative profitability of a business from the business's point of view. Usually calculated as profit before tax and interest/total assets–current liabilities. Note that there are many other definitions.

Return on equity (ROE)

Or return on shareholders' funds (ROSF). A commonly used ratio in financial analysis that gives some indication of the relative profitability of a business from the shareholders' point of view. Usually calculated as profit after tax and interest/shareholders funds. Note that there are many other definitions. (See **return on capital employed**.)

Revenue

American accounting term for sales, turnover or income.

Revenue expenditure

Short-term expenditure that is written off to the income statement (profit and loss account) each year. It has nothing to do with **revenue**. (See **capital expenditure**.)

Sales
See **turnover**.

Share capital and share premium account
In the **balance sheet**, share capital (common stock) represents the nominal value of the shares in the business purchased by the original **shareholders** (stockholders). If they paid a premium on the nominal value of their shares, the difference appears in the share premium account (capital surplus or additional paid-in capital in the United States).

Shareholders
Often, though not always, called stockholders in the United States. In theory they are the owners of a business – though in big listed businesses they tend to behave more like the owners of **capital**, as if the share is what they own rather than a slice of the business. There are two main types of shareholders:

- Ordinary shareholders share in the profits and **losses** and have voting rights. They may receive income in the form of **dividends**, but not until interest has been paid to **debt holders**.

- Preferred or preference shareholders come in many forms depending on the business, but essentially they have rights not available to ordinary shareholders, including the right to receive dividends and capital distributions before the ordinary shareholders. They generally do not have voting rights, though preferred ordinary shareholders may well do. Preferred shares are often used as part of financing mechanisms provided by venture capitalists. ("Preferred" and "preference" are usually used interchangeably, though sometimes preference is used to describe a share or stock that is junior in terms of rights to a preferred one.)

See Chapter 6.

Shareholders' equity
See below.

Shareholders' funds

Sometimes shareholders' equity or equity account in the United States. The shareholders' financial interest in a business (this is not the same as the value of the business). The amount can be calculated either by working out the business's net assets, or by adding together the **share capital, share premium account, retained profits** and other distributable reserves.

Share or stock options

The right to buy shares (stocks in the United States) in a company at a predetermined price regardless of the value of the shares at the time the options are exercised. Incentive schemes for directors often include options.
See Chapter 7.

Sole trader

Where many businesses start.

SME

Short for small and medium-sized enterprise, variously defined by different agencies.

Staff promotion

One of the most misunderstood and mishandled management processes. People who are good at their current job may not be good at a job higher up; and people who are bad at their current job may do well at a higher level (though, of course, they will not get the opportunity to show this).

Stock

There are many meanings. Some are as follows:

- On the **balance sheet** in the UK, it refers to goods bought for resale or components bought for assembly. In a manufacturing business, it can also refer to the amount of work in progress and finished goods waiting for sale, and thus includes direct labour costs and other direct costs as well as materials. In the United States the term used is inventory.

- In the United States it is a common term for shares.
- In the UK it can mean the same as bond, a tradable form of debt as opposed to a share.

Strategy

One of those words used by those purporting to know a lot about businesses but who might struggle to define it clearly. For some, business strategy is almost synonymous with management and gets confused with tactics. For others, it is all about formal ways of thinking about the big picture and putting together grand plans to get there. Businesses ambitious about growth stand a better chance of achieving it if they take business strategy, however defined, seriously. Perhaps the most succinct definition is given by Gerry Johnson and Kevan Scholes:[28] "Strategy is the direction and scope of an organisation over the long term: which achieves advantage for the organisation through its configuration of resources within a challenging environment, to meet the needs of markets and to fulfil stakeholder expectations." See Chapters 3 and 4.

Subsidiary company

When one business owns the whole of another business, or has effective control of it, the latter business is a subsidiary of the former. (See **consolidated statement**.)

Succession

One of those processes that most businesses give little thought to until it is too late. In **family businesses**, for example, it is easy to see that succession (or rather transfer from one generation to another) is a matter of corporate life or death (the majority do not survive to the third generation). But for any owner-manager the issues can be just as serious. In a business that is dependent on its owner, succession planning is essential if the owner wants to hand it on or sell it and extract some sort of value. See Chapter 7.

Sustainable growth

Many profitable businesses get into trouble because they grow too quickly, or rather because the managers worry too much about getting in new business and not enough about generating cash quickly enough to pay the bills. A growing business consumes a lot more cash than is often anticipated, and that cash has to come from somewhere. If the business does not generate the cash, it will have to come from outside.

See Chapter 6.

Tax

Whatever your views about tax, two principles are worth keeping in mind:

■ Saving tax is rarely the prime objective of a business, so always determine what the business objectives are and then establish the most tax effective way of delivering them, not the other way round.

■ The tax authorities will be ever watchful. Once lost, their trust is hard to regain.

Team

Simply putting a group of people together and telling them they are a team is likely to result in the sum of the efforts of the individual members being less than if you had left them alone in the first place. Without attention to the team itself, a group of people – particularly ambitious managers – are likely to tread on each other's toes. Team construction and management takes time, effort and money. What is important is that there is a good reason for forming a team in the first place, that it is put together intelligently and managed well.

The enormous range of tasks that need to be done in a growing business means many **entrepreneurs** are in effect teams rather than individuals. Indeed, there is evidence to suggest that businesses founded by teams of individuals grow faster than those founded by individuals. (See **management team**.)

See Chapter 7.

Trade sale

A term used when a business is sold to another business rather than to a group of financial investors. A business for sale is usually worth more to a trade buyer in the same industry than to anyone else because such a buyer is likely to be able to achieve synergies.

Turnover

Sales revenue. The "top line" in the income statement or profit and loss account in the financial statements. Also called income or revenue.

Valuation

In theory, the value of a **listed company** is the price its shares sell for on the stockmarket, although a potential buyer of the whole company will usually have to pay more to persuade sufficient numbers of **shareholders** to sell. Valuing a private company is more difficult. Where a value needs to be determined other than through negotiation, the process will need to be conducted by an agreed specialist who will, in the case of a sale of a minority shareholding, put a lower value on the share price than if the whole company is sold. This can result in unhappiness on the part of those wanting to untangle their involvement in a business. Otherwise, it is generally worth remembering that something is worth what someone else is prepared to pay for it – no more, no less.

Venture capital

Venture capitalists look for high return and are prepared to take high risk. They invest money they raise from investors in a portfolio of businesses that they hope will grow rapidly. Venture capitalists aim to realise their investments in a shortish term (around five years), usually by selling the investments on or refinancing them in some way, keeping some of the gains themselves and distributing the rest among the investing partners.
See Chapter 6.

Weighted average cost of capital

Or WACC, the average return required by investors in a business. If a business is to succeed, in the long run its profits must exceed the cost of capital. Working out this cost means calculating the cost of the equity and taking the actual average interest rate on the debt. These two charges are then weighted according to the proportion of equity and debt in the total capital.

Working capital

The financial resources tied up in the day-to-day operation of a business, or the money tied up in goods and services that have been or are waiting to be made or sold. The bigger the business the more money needs to be tied up in working capital. The need to finance working capital often puts unexpected financial pressure on a growing business.

See Chapter 6.

Notes and further reading

1 *Financial Times*, April 19th 2002.
2 Flamholtz, G. and Randle, Y., *Growing Pains: Transitioning from an Entrepreneurship to a Professionally Managed Firm*, Jossey Bass, 2000.
3 Baghai, M., Coley, S. and White, D., *The Alchemy of Growth: Practical Insights for Building the Enduring Enterprise*, Basic Books, 2000.
4 Sull, D., *The Upside of Turbulence: Seizing Opportunity in an Uncertain World*, Collins Business, 2009.
5 Champion, D. and Carr, N., "Starting up in high gear: An interview with venture capitalist Vinod Khosla", *Harvard Business Review*, July 2000.
6 Barker, E., "Start with Nothing", *Inc. Magazine*, February 2002.
7 Quoted by Amar Bhidé in *The Origin and Evolution of New Businesses*, Oxford University Press, 2000.
8 Moore, G., *Crossing the Chasm: Marketing and Selling Technology Products to Mainstream Customers*, HarperBusiness, 1991. There have been various editions and revisions.
9 Zook, C. and Allen, J., *Profit from the Core: Growth Strategy in an Era of Turbulence*, Harvard Business School Press, 2001.
10 Zook, C., *Beyond the Core: Expand Your Market Without Abandoning Your Roots*, Harvard Business School Press, 2003.
11 Ansoff, I., "Strategies for Diversification", *Harvard Business Review*, September 1957.
12 Porter, M., *Competitive Strategy: Techniques for Analyzing Industries and Competitors*, The Free Press, 1980.

13 Stangler, D., "The Economic Future Just Happened", Ewing Marion Kauffman Foundation, June 2009.

14 Quoted by Charles Handy in *The New Alchemists*, Hutchinson, 1999.

15 Stangler, D., op. cit.

16 Katzenbach, J.R. and Smith, D.K., *The Wisdom of Teams: Creating the High-Performance Organization*, HarperBusiness, 1994.

17 Simons, R., "How risky is your company?", *Harvard Business Review*, May 1999.

18 Kaplan, R. and Norton, D., "Using the Balanced Scorecard as a Strategic Management System", *Harvard Business Review*, January 1996; and *The Balanced Scorecard: translating strategy into action*, Harvard Business School Press, 1996.

19 Katzenbach and Smith, op. cit.

20 Capron, L. and Mitchell, W., "Finding the Right Path", *Harvard Business Review*, July 2010.

21 Harding, D. and Rovit, S., "Building Deals on Bedrock", *Harvard Business Review*, January 2004.

22 Rosabeth Moss Kanter blog, June 1st 2010.

23 Baghai, M., Coley, S. and White, D., op. cit.

24 Downes, L. and Mui, C., *Unleashing the Killer App: Digital Strategies for Market Dominance*, Harvard Business School Press, 1998.

25 Adam Smith (1759), *The Theory of Moral Sentiments*, Knud Haakonssen (ed.), Cambridge University Press, 2002, p. 222.

26 Hamel, G. and Prahalad, C.K., *Competing for the Future*, Harvard Business School Press, 1994.

27 Brandenburger, A. and Nalebuff, B., *Co-Opetition*, Currency Doubleday, 1996.

28 Johnson, G. and Scholes, K., *Exploring Corporate Strategy*, 7th edn, Financial Times/Prentice Hall, 2006.

Further reading

Adizes, I., *Managing Corporate Lifecycles*, revised edition, Prentice Hall Press, 1999.

Barrow, G., Burke, L., Clarke, D. and Molian, P., *Growing your Business: A Handbook for Ambitious Owner-managers*, Routledge, 2008.

Drucker, P., *Innovation and Entrepreneurship*, revised edition, Butterworth-Heinemann, 1994.

Grundy, T., *Breakthrough Strategies for Growth*, Financial Times/ Prentice Hall, 1995.

Komisar, R., *The Monk and the Riddle: The Art of Creating a Life While Making a Living*, Harvard Business Press, 2001.

Merson, R., *Rules are Not Enough: The art of governance in the real world*, Profile Books, 2010.

Mullins, J. and Komisar, R., *Getting to Plan B: Breaking Through to a Better Business Model*, Harvard Business School Press, 2009.

Porter, M.E., *On Competition*, updated edition, Harvard Business School Press, 2008.

Timmons, J.A. and Spinelli, S., *New Venture Creation: Entrepreneurship for the 21st Century*, 8th edition, McGraw-Hill Higher Education, 2008.

Index